The Professional's Guide to Business Development

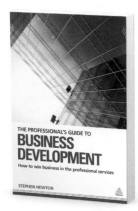

The Professional's Guide to Business Development

How to win business in the professional services

Stephen Newton

KoganPage

LONDON PHILADELPHIA NEW DELHI

First published in Great Britain and the United States in 2013 by Kogan Page Limited

120 Pentonville Road	1518 Walnut Street, Suite 1100	4737/23 Ansari Road
London N1 9JN	Philadelphia PA 19102	Daryaganj
United Kingdom	USA	New Delhi 110002
www.koganpage.com		India

© Stephen Newton, 2013

ISBN   978 0 7494 6653 4
E-ISBN 978 0 7494 6654 1

British Library Cataloguing-in-Publication Data

A CIP record for this book is available from the British Library.

Library of Congress Cataloging-in-Publication Data

Newton, Stephen.
    The professional's guide to business development : how to win business in the professional services / Stephen Newton.
        p. cm.
    ISBN 978-0-7494-6653-4 – ISBN 978-0-7494-6654-1   1. Professions.   2. Branding (Marketing)
3. Small business–Management.   4. Success in business.   I. Title.
    HD8038.A1N49 2012
    658–dc23
                                                                                    2012029000

Typeset by Graphicraft Limited, Hong Kong
Printed and bound in India by Replika Press Pvt Ltd

CONTENTS

ACKNOWLEDGEMENTS

I would like to record my appreciation of some of the organizations and individuals that have been important to me and influential in the writing of this book.

The British Army was a formative influence in my early career. It taught me the value of planning and organization and of defining the results you seek so that you minimize the impact of chance (which is so often negative) in achieving them. I also learned that 'flexibility is next to Godliness' plus the value of punctuality, concurrent activity and of allocating time meticulously. Time is a finite and precious resource and this life is sometimes unexpectedly short. The Army sent me to University, something that was entirely unexpected and for which I am unremittingly grateful – especially as it was an unusual step at the time.

At University I experienced the joy of exploring multiple possibilities and of being comfortable with the need for uncertainty whilst you arrive at a position from which certainty can be achieved. I also came to understand the meaning of the term 'seriously bright people'.

Mercury Asset Management (MAM) was still run 'in the Warburg way' during my time there, which meant that 'I's were invariably dotted and 'T's crossed. Sound judgement was valued over short-term profit. My colleagues at MAM comprised the most talented group of people with whom I have worked at any one time.

With my own children, Emily and Benjamin, I experienced the absolute joy and pride of parenthood and the need to allow others to reach their own conclusions, no matter how uncomfortable. From my parents, now both dead, I learned that no matter how hard one might try one cannot ensure the happiness of another, nor is one responsible for it.

From my future step-daughter, Olivia Barr, I learned that the best of things often come to those who are patient. With my fiancé, Poppy Barr, I found peace and safe haven and my best friend.

Anne Scoular of Meyler Campbell taught me to coach. She was the first person to tell me that I could 'listen like a bat' and came up with the marvellous description of active listening as 'listening to understand rather than simply to respond'. She has been, for over a decade, a constant support in my business and is someone with whom I hope to work more in the future.

Nathan Mobley III of Andover Partners LLC in Darien, Connecticut, introduced me to the 'Andover Magic' which underlies some of the ideas in this book. He was one of the first people to encourage me simply to 'be myself' in business and introduced me to the power of conversation and the use of silence. He helped me to get my life back following my divorce and was generous in opening his home, his friendships and his experience to me.

Last but by no means least, the incomparable Liz Gooster, Editor-At-Large at Kogan Page, encouraged me to write this book and made sure that it was readable.

Thanks to you all.

Stephen Newton

Introduction

To succeed in the field of professional services you need the ability to become a strategic entrepreneur who happens to be a technical expert, not simply a technical expert who happens to apply that expertise as a consultant, lawyer, accountant, banker, etc. That implies rethinking the way we work and in particular the way we use time, ensuring that we focus on working with the 'right' clients, where we can help the client to win and thus win ourselves. It means a strong focus on the development of personal relationships with those clients.

It means introducing systems and structure into every part of our business, and in particular into the marketing and sales processes, to build and grow your professional practice. Regardless of its size, each part of your business must operate in support of the brand on which your marketing and selling are founded. Each of us is required to understand that no amount of technical expertise matters unless it can be sold to a willing buyer and delivered in a manner that is profitable for both parties.

Too many professionals think of technical expertise as a differentiating factor in the mind of clients. Experience indicates that, by and large, it is not; it is assumed – a hygiene factor. If the client did not believe that you have the expertise to deliver a given piece of work you would not get through the door. The client assumes that you have the necessary capability in the same way that we all assume that the pilot of a commercial airliner can fly the plane. The client will hire you based on many other factors.

We need to ensure that we understand not simply what the client 'needs' at a commercial level, but what drives the key players within the client firm at a deep emotional level, which is where decisions are taken. We need to be able to find out where there may be a 'commercial fit' that allows us an opportunity to work with a given client and to articulate the value that we, uniquely, can bring to solving that problem or fulfilling that dream.

We need to talk in language that resonates with the client as an individual, because there is no such thing as a company, only people. We need to be able to engender a basic connection with a potential client at a personal, human level – I call this establishing 'like and trust' or L+T, and we explore some of the factors that support this throughout this book.

Without basic L+T, it will be unlikely if not impossible that we can do business with the client. The establishment of L+T allows us to develop the relationship to the point where the client seeks to buy rather than needing to be sold to. Once the initial small step is taken we must enhance the relationship to the point where we become a business partner in the true sense: where the client sees us as a necessary and critical path to success.

None of the above should come as a surprise. It is, surely, just good practice. Indeed. However, it is not necessarily *common* practice. Why? Because too few individuals in the professional services industries have taken the trouble to develop a repeatable methodology to do these things consistently and fewer still use it routinely. Few take the time to plan and to use a systematic approach to the development of their business and growth of their practice.

This book provides a toolkit and a methodology to enable you to do all of the above consistently. The result – if you follow the approach – will be to transform the way in which you go about your business. Your success rate will increase exponentially.

How to begin?

Choosing your ground

Water shapes its course according to the nature of the ground over which it flows. (SUN TZU – *THE ART OF WAR*)

People in the professions tend to define themselves in terms of their specific professional expertise (lawyer, accountant, banker, consultant, etc) rather than in terms of the needs and wants of the client and of their desired role with the client. Clients consequently see those in professional services as 'suppliers' or 'service providers'. They will only rarely differentiate between them on grounds other than price. In the mind of the client, professional expertise is usually assumed: it is no more than a hygiene factor. Expertise is therefore a necessary but not a sufficient factor in winning business. For professionals to seek to win clients' business as the 'low bidder' is a sure way to kill their own business.

My experience indicates that clients will buy (whether from you or from your competitors) only when they are ready to do so. They will buy only from those individuals for whom they feel a basic liking and where that liking leads to inherent trust (L+T) at both a personal and a professional level. Clients will do business with you because they can visualize and understand specific benefits to themselves from working with you and not because of the 'features' of your product or service.

Their decision to buy will normally be made to resolve a felt problem or to fulfil a dream. The type of solution as well as the specific results needed to resolve that problem or fulfil that dream will usually exist in the client's mind (at least at a conceptual level) before any action is taken to find a provider of the solution. In most cases, buying decisions are made at an emotional level and justified subsequently by logic. Firms do not take these buying decisions: people do. Therefore 'a firm' is only the shorthand name for the individuals that comprise it – there is no such thing as 'a firm' when it comes to decision making, only people.

Failure to understand and to act upon these self-evident truths lies at the root of most business development problems in the professions and indeed elsewhere. This book provides you with a repeatable and scalable approach to address these potential problems and to:

- qualify clients so that you focus your efforts where they are most likely to succeed;
- get in front of the right people more of the time;
- enable potential clients to find and approach you and to do so before they even consider a Request for Proposal (an RFP) or 'beauty parade', so that you maximize the likelihood of winning business and developing your relationship from a position of strength;
- develop and foster excellent long-term relationships so that you minimize price as a selection factor in doing business with you, maximize your share of each client's available budget in your field and minimize competition;
- find out rapidly and with a high degree of accuracy what drives each individual client at a deep emotional level and how they prefer to receive information;
- move from making presentations and selling services to holding conversations and addressing known and relevant needs, thus enabling the client to agree to a solution rather than persuading them to buy your idea;
- use meetings to gather information and propose solutions, not simply as selling vehicles, so that you advance your perceived role in the eyes of the client from 'Just Another ...' to that of trusted business partner;
- move the level of your client relationships up the pyramid from a transactional/commodity basis (where price and speed of delivery are key drivers) to 'external team member' where you are recognized as a critical enabler of the client's success and make a real and measurable contribution to their business, as well as your own (see Chapter 7 for more on the relationship pyramid);
- adopt a strategic account leadership approach rather than a sales-led approach to business development. This will allow you to share in the client's business planning processes, to recognize and point out to the client opportunities that are of mutual relevance and benefit, and become embedded in the execution of those opportunities. This in turn further cements your relationship and engenders platinum references and referrals, internally within the client firm and externally to non-competitors.

This approach has been field-tested over more than a decade and can be used by any professional, regardless of their specific calling: indeed it has been shown to work in many fields outside the professional services industry.

Its focus is not on enhancing your professional expertise but on identifying the 'best' clients for you, understanding what 'makes clients tick', identifying the 'commercial fit' (or opportunity for you to work with the client in a manner that is profitable to both of you), articulating clearly how your unique value benefits the individual client and focusing on those clients where you are able to build the most mutually valuable relationships. Note the word choice: *mutually* valuable. The relationship has to work on a two-way basis because it is only then that mutual respect and a partnership of equals is engendered, as opposed to a 'buyer/supplier' (or 'win/lose') relationship, which is inherently less satisfactory.

New business versus business development

It is common sense to seek to play where you have the greatest likelihood of winning. Where possible you would naturally seek to play the game that best suits your temperament, skills and attributes. Military commanders have always sought to fight over ground that suits their forces and to position their forces to take advantage of the chosen ground. In the professional services arena, this begins with identifying the type of client with whom you feel best able to be successful and forming a realistic view of the strengths and vulnerabilities of your offering *as seen by the client*.

Many professionals will seek to win new business from *any* available new client, rather than developing relationships with existing ones or seeking opportunities to work with *carefully selected* new clients. However, research indicates that it costs up to seven times more to win a new client than to win additional business from an existing one. Experience indicates that not all clients, new or existing, represent good business opportunities and that many sales professionals feel that up to a third of their client base is non-profitable, at best.

Understanding objectively which of your clients is profitable and, for those that are not currently, what can be done to make them profitable for you, will help you to avoid wasting time and effort. It is also an opportunity to examine the 'enjoyment factor': do you *like* working with particular clients (or not). If you enjoy working with a client, there is a good chance that they feel the same. This is the basis for developing a good relationship that eventually moves up the pyramid and has several benefits, as we will explore later.

Many professionals will chase short-term revenue wins. The result is that they often win a tactical battle but lose the war to a competitor who focuses on the development of long-term relationships at the expense of short-term gain. Those who take the short view on immediate revenue will also find that, in many cases, the 'one-off special introductory price' becomes the basis for further downward negotiation.

One of the benefits of the exercises we shall undertake during this and subsequent chapters is to gain an objective view not only of where you can be most successful but where not to play, so that you can focus your efforts on winning business that you want, where the result is mutual benefit – ie for both you and for your client.

There is often an assumption that sheer volume of sales activity, 'pushing products and services hard enough' will drive improved revenue. This is a transactional, 'hunter-gatherer' approach, as opposed to a 'farming' approach. Conventional wisdom has it that professionals should seek to become 'farmers' of their business relationships and leave behind the hunter-gatherer approach. The reality is that neither approach is uniquely 'right'. While it is important to avoid confusing activity with progress, it is essential to seek some new opportunities to replace the natural attrition that occurs in business relationships over time due to organizational changes, movement of key clients within or between firms, etc.

Where are you?

In Lewis Carroll's *Alice in Wonderland*, Alice asks the caterpillar which way she should go. The caterpillar asks where she wants to get to. Alice says that it doesn't much matter, to which the caterpillar replies that it therefore matters little which way she goes. But 'where to go' or 'which way' are poor questions until you can understand where you are and, more important, where your potential clients perceive you to be, both in absolute terms and relative to competitors. In this context, 'where you are' includes several factors:

- The current macro-economic situation (as it affects your own business, your clients' business and the business of their clients).
- Your clients'/potential clients' individual economic situation and your own (business model, external pressures, etc; the factors that would inform a business SWOT analysis).
- Your current offering/expertise and how it may uniquely benefit both existing and potential clients and also their customers or clients.
- How the client perceives you and your role with them.

In assessing these factors, it is hardly ever sensible to assume either unalloyed joy or desperation. Neither is likely to represent reality for long. As a Rabbi of my acquaintance says, 'Good or ill, this too shall pass.'

It is unlikely that you will be able to change these factors in the near term. You must therefore understand current reality and work with it rather than against it, in much the same way as a gardener tests the composition of the soil so as to understand what plants will thrive and which are likely to fail. The composition of soil can be changed over time, by adding chemicals or mulch. Plants can be grown in a container of imported compost of the required type.

Either way, the gardener prepares ground that is suitable for the plants he or she wishes to grow or adapts the choice of plants to the type of soil available.

Similarly, business development for the professional should begin not with frenzied, seed-sowing activity but with the selection and preparation of ground on which you can most likely win, given the resources at your disposal and the results you seek to achieve. The benefit is to conserve and focus two of your most important assets: time and money. Of the two, the former is, in my view, the more important because it is by definition finite and non-fungible. Money can be leveraged and re-allocated. Time can be used only once. It can be leveraged only by bringing together groups of individuals in the form of teams working to achieve a common purpose: more of that later in Chapter 10.

It pays to take time to assess and to plan before you start any business development activity. If your current business development approach involves responding to any RFP that comes your way, regardless of how tight the deadline for responses, or simply approaching as many organizations as possible to gain agreement to an initial meeting, stop. Take time to assess where you are in terms of your current client relationships and positioning of your business and then decide where you want to get to with current clients and the type of clients with whom you would prefer to work. In other words, design your business from the desired end-state backwards. Only then can you decide the general direction of travel; it will usually be hard to plan the whole journey in detail. The planning process need not take long – nor should it if you are to avoid planning paralysis.

You may be sceptical of taking time to plan and gather data. As General Eisenhower said, 'No plan survives contact with the enemy. Plans themselves are of little use. However, the process of planning is vital.' Acting with no plan, or at least with no clear aim in mind and uncertainty about where you stand, is doomed to failure.

Seeing the ground from the client's position

It is essential that you view the world through the eyes of your clients, at least in the first instance, rather than solely through your own. It is their reality that matters first and foremost. Their perception of the situation may not be the same as yours but it is reality for them and will be hard to alter. It will be easier to accept the client's perceptions as a starting point, if nothing more.

The Charge of the Light Brigade is one of the best-known instances of a disaster that stemmed from two commanders seeing the same piece of ground from different positions. From his vantage point high up on the west side of the valley down which the Light Brigade would eventually advance, Lord Raglan, the overall commander of British forces at the time, could see the Russians manoeuvring to take away captured naval guns that lay in a redoubt behind a fold in the ground on the southern side of the valley. He wanted

British cavalry to advance with a view to preventing the removal of those naval guns.

Lord Lucan, overall commander of the British cavalry and stationed on the valley floor, received the order to advance from Raglan and passed it to the Earl of Cardigan, commanding the five regiments of the Light Brigade who were also positioned on the valley floor. Both Lucan and Raglan could see only the Russian batteries positioned at the end of the valley approximately a mile and a quarter away, and not the activity around the captured naval guns. Raglan's order to 'advance rapidly to the front and try to prevent the Russians taking away the guns' was consequently unclear from their standpoint. The Light Brigade advanced into the face of the Russian batteries and was decimated.

Your planning should be informed by a realistic (and if possible an informed) view of how the client sees the ground over which you both operate.

In theory, you may be able to provide a set of services to any individual or firm. In reality you can be successful with only a relatively small number. The more closely you can define the type of firm and the type of individual that you can best serve, the easier it will become to identify what potential clients may see as your particular strengths and indeed where they may feel your offering is weaker. The more closely you can define the 'perfect client' for you, the easier it becomes to develop strategies to identify and locate the specific clients with whom you can be most successful. We examine the way to 'qualify' clients in more detail in Chapter 2.

If you have an existing client base, you can begin to assess where you are through the eyes of what you consider your best or most important clients. That does not necessarily mean those clients that provide the greatest proportion of today's revenue, although that may be a reasonable starting point. If you have no current clients (for example because you have only recently started your business) you will need to carry out an initial assessment in the abstract. You should review it in the light of experience. Indeed I recommend that this type of exercise is carried out at least annually in any event.

Macro-economic situation

The data you will need to complete this exercise can be found easily online and indeed you need look no further than FT.com to locate the majority of it. You may wish to look at additional sources of data and calculate an average of the results you see. In my view, this adds undue complexity. The purpose of the exercise is to ensure that you and your team have a common understanding of the context in which you and your potential clients operate. You need to assess trends rather than carry out detailed analysis. What you are looking for is an understanding of any impacts, positive or negative, of the current and likely future situation on your client's and hence on your own business environment. The relevant basic data needed can be added to Table 1.1.

TABLE 1.1 Macro-economic review

Economic indicator	Current	1 Year ago	Projection/ trend over next year	What does that indicate? What could be potential 'commercial fits' or opportunities in your field of expertise?
GDP growth – annualized (for your client's primary market)				Higher GDP indicates potential for increased spending and that companies may be in 'growth mode'. Potential for new development projects, financing opportunities and organizational change. Lower GDP indicates cost constraint for companies and individuals. Opportunities to streamline operations, outsource, dispose of non-core assets, improve sales and/or margins.
GDP growth – annualized (for your own country or region)				
Interest rates (bank base rate) for your client's primary location				Higher interest rates indicate increased inflation and financing costs. Opportunities to save cost. Lower interest rates indicate lower financing cost so greater propensity to invest. May be good short to medium term but beware any indication of lower demand. Compare interest rates to inflation rate (CPI/RPI). If inflation is higher, real value of cash is falling. Opportunity to invest in capital projects.
Interest rates (bank base rate) for your own location				
Oil price (eg Brent Crude)				High oil price indicates either strong demand or reduced production. Key is to understand which and why that has occurred. High oil price impacts transport costs. Opportunity to reduce consumption and save cost as well as boost 'green' credentials.

TABLE 1.1 *continued*

Economic indicator	Current	1 Year ago	Projection/trend over next year	What does that indicate? What could be potential 'commercial fits' or opportunities in your field of expertise?
Other commodity prices that may be relevant to the client				High prices indicate higher input costs. Good for producers, not so good for consumers. Opportunities to reduce volumes required by improved manufacturing processes or adoption of new technology.
Currency exchange rate ($/£)				Strong currency means lower import cost but higher export cost. Opportunity to stabilize rates by hedging, etc, review suppliers, agree fixed rate contracts, relocate manufacturing facilities, outsource production, etc or refocus sales effort on domestic/overseas markets as appropriate.
Currency exchange rate (€/£)				
Other currency exchange rates that may be relevant to the client				
Price/Earnings ratio for the main equity index in the client's location				Lower P/E indicates either that share prices are cheap or that earnings are projected to fall. Need to examine why current P/E differs from long-term average. Opportunity to reduce cost base, outsource, adopt better technology, move from fixed to variable costs, improve sales and/or margins.
Price/Earnings ratio for the main equity index in your own location				

Questions to ask based on the data are:

- Is the picture broadly positive or negative for your clients and for you?
- What opportunities (if any) could this information highlight for your clients?
- How could you leverage the unique strengths of you and your team to enable the client to make the most of those opportunities?
- What weaknesses could it highlight in your client's current business model?
- How can you and your team use your unique strengths to help to minimize the impact of those weaknesses?

Client firm's economic situation (and your own)

This second exercise drills down into the factors that affect your clients at the organizational level. It will be important subsequently to consider the situation of the key players within the client firm – as I said earlier, there is no such thing as a firm, only people. However, at this stage you are looking to understand the context in which the individuals operate in order to identify what opportunities there may be for a commercial fit between you and your firm and the client.

I recommend that you carry out the same exercise for your own firm to assess as objectively as possible your relative strengths. This exercise is equally relevant whether your firm is a major multinational or a one-person operation. The fact that you operate as a sole proprietor need not rule you out from working with major organizations. I routinely win business from major firms in diverse industries.

Table 1.2 sets out a series of questions. The answers should be given using a scale of your choice. I suggest a simple 1–10 scale where 10 is high. The current rating represents your assessment of the client's position today. The desired rating represents the level at which the client would need to operate to become or to remain one of the 'winners' in its field over the coming two to three years. Think in terms of a 'bell curve' rating (Figure 1.1) where a rating of 9 indicates a level better than 98 per cent of competitors and where approximately 50 per cent of ratings would fall between 4 and 6.

As we will find in Chapter 2, one of the factors that will influence your choice of clients is their likely future strength. It may be that you can help a client to improve its relative strength, and therein lies an opportunity for you. If it is not immediately clear that you can do so or how to do so, this should be an alarm signal.

The traffic light approach (red, amber, green, where red is negative and green is positive) is designed to provide an easily understood picture of where the client stands so that you can assess both opportunities and risks, and how best to approach them. Use a 'green' for current ratings of 6 and above and a red for those either currently at or below 4 or where the

TABLE 1.2   Client's micro-economic position review

Issue	Current rating (1–10)	Desired rating (1–10)	Traffic light rating
Is the industry in which the client operates growing or consolidating?			
Is the client's position/competitive advantage within its industry improving or declining?			
Does the client have a strong balance sheet relative to others in its industry?			
Are the client's sales growing in absolute terms?			
Are the client's sales growing relative to others in its industry?			
Are the client's profit margins strong relative to others in its industry?			
Is the client seen as a leader in its industry – 'the one to beat' either in terms of products and services or in more general terms?			
Is the client widely recognized as having good people, effective leaders and good development approaches for its people?			
Is the client firm widely recognized as a 'good place to work'?			

difference between current and desired ratings is 2 or more. Experience indicates that it is hard to close a gap much larger than this within a reasonable timeframe. Where you have 'reds' you will need to develop an action plan to move them to at least 'ambers'. If there are more than three 'reds', this represents an alarm signal.

The financial data needed to complete the first few sections can be found in the statutory report and accounts of a limited company (available from Companies House in the UK). If the company is listed on a stock exchange, the data will be available from sources such as Hoovers (**www.hoovers.com**)

FIGURE 1.1 A bell curve

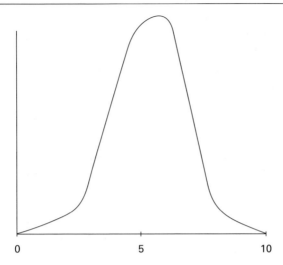

or Thomson Reuters. For partnerships, the data may be less easy to access but much can be gleaned from information available via the relevant trade press or professional association. For example, the weekly newspaper for the UK legal profession, *The Lawyer*, publishes a variety of reports including an annual listing of revenue and profit data for the top 200 UK legal firms. The websites of individual firms sometimes carry an astonishing amount of data on financials, people and positioning.

Some of the issues require an element of subjective judgement or assessment. If you are not able to make an estimate in which you feel reasonably confident, this should raise a red flag that you may not yet know enough about the client firm to enable you to assess potential opportunities.

Based on the information in Table 1.2, you can now think about the following questions:

- Is the picture broadly positive or negative for your clients (and for you)?
- What opportunities or problems could this information highlight (if any)? (Don't forget that a possible problem for a client may represent an opportunity for you.) How might these enable the client to enhance its position with its clients/customers?
- How could you leverage the unique strengths of you and your team to enable the client to make the most of those opportunities or overcome the problems?
- Where do you feel that you and your team may best be able to establish a good commercial fit that you are not yet exploiting?
- Is there a real opportunity with this client? If so, is it real for you: can you win?

Your current offering and how the client sees you

We will explore this set of issues in more detail in Chapter 4. However, at this point, it is necessary simply to explore what you see as your strengths and possible vulnerabilities and how they are seen by clients. The benefit is to help you to focus on those areas where you can maximize the degree of 'fit' with potential clients and minimize the amount of time wasted in chasing opportunities that are in fact illusory. In other words, it helps to ensure a firm grasp on reality. This also acts as a precursor to the exercise in Chapter 4 designed to define your unique value.

There are two sets of questions to consider: why should the client hire you, and how does the client perceive you and your role with them? The first is a variation of 'What makes you different?' or, 'What is your USP?' It seeks to focus not on what you do as a profession (accountant, consultant, etc) nor on what factors might make you technically 'better' than others, but on the softer factors that could help a client to choose you rather than others. In this context factors such as attention to detail, high levels of output, lower cost, etc are not really relevant and indeed to focus on this kind of factor can be damaging to your brand. Clients will usually take such things as a given and may feel that 'methinks he doth protest too much' if you focus on them as differentiators. At this point, we are not seeking to clarify or develop a USP statement for you: we do that in Chapter 4. The aim is to understand how clients perceive you and your role with them today and then to contrast that view with the way you would like it to be so that you can be most successful in developing your business. Later, this may include dropping certain clients.

A good way to find some initial answers to both of the above questions is, believe it or not, simply to ask your current clients for their input. Most will be happy to be asked and will appreciate you taking time to gain their input. If they are not it can be a signal that the relationship is not as good as you thought. You can use questions like:

- What was the most important factor for you in deciding to hire me?
- What could I do more of, less of, differently or better, to reinforce that view?
- In what ways do you feel we can work together most effectively in the future?
- How do you now see my role in working with you and your firm?

The nature and quality of the answers will tell you a lot about how the client takes buying decisions. You will also begin to see how the client perceives your role as well as how far up the relationship pyramid you currently stand. You will gain some insight as to whether the client looks on you simply as an outsourced provider of specific professional expertise (essentially at the transactional or commodity level) or as an external business partner – or something in between.

At the lowest level, we have the supplier of a commodity. In that role your keys to success lie in price and speed/certainty of delivery. At the upper end of the pyramid we have those who are considered by the client as a true business partner, but one who happens not to be employed by the same organization (although you may have a desk in their offices and spend considerable time there). Your keys to success in that role lie in:

- the depth of understanding you are perceived to have of the client's business and business issues,
- the perceived strength of your relationship with key players both in the client firm and in your own (so that you can bring to bear the resources needed to deliver the best solutions); and
- your perceived willingness to contribute to the development of their business (in helping to build the client's business you will ultimately build your own).

The focus is on strength of relationships and depth of understanding rather than on periodic sales/revenue targets. Note also the use of the word 'perceived'. It is not objective fact that matters here but the way the client perceives their relationship with you.

Some of the responses you receive as to the reason the client hired you may sound surprising initially. One senior banker I know heard from a client that he had been hired to deliver a major IPO because he would be more fun to work with than the competitors and not because he was thought to be 'better qualified' than they were. As we will explore later, decisions are taken largely on emotional grounds and justified subsequently by logic.

Based on conversations you have with clients or on your own observations you can begin to complete Table 1.3 with data on clients' views of your own position. Compile one table for each client. In each case try to look at what the client believes rather than what you believe or would like to be the case. As before, rate each factor on a scale of 1 to 10 with 10 being high, and think in terms of a bell-curve ranking. Allocate a 'red' traffic light rating where the current rating is 4 or less (or where the difference between current and desired ratings is 2 or more), green for current ratings of 7 or more and amber for others.

Assessing the data

You should now have three sets of data for each client:

1 a macro-economic review;
2 a micro-economic review; and
3 a client perceptions review.

TABLE 1.3   Client perceptions exercise

Factor	Current rating	Desired rating	Red, amber or green?
My view of my role with the client and theirs are fully aligned. (Write a one-sentence description and test it with the client if in any doubt.)			
The client sees a clear difference between my service/offering and those of competitors and can describe it clearly.			
The client identifies the same competitors as I do in my field.			
My and the client's assessment of the current and desired levels of our relationship are aligned.			
I have a clear understanding of the business issues that affect this client and his industry and consequent opportunities for this client.			
I see how my firm's strengths can help this client to achieve success in exploiting these opportunities.			
I recognize the relevant weaknesses of my offering for this client and can see ways to mitigate them.			
The client is able to articulate clear benefits that I bring in working with him (or her).			
Both the client and I enjoy our working relationship and have fun when working together.			
The client and I would be happy to meet socially outside the work environment.			

If possible carry out the client perceptions exercise for each individual within the client firm and not just for the firm as a whole. You are likely to find different perceptions in some key areas for each person.

For each client, you can now assess:

- the overall context in which you and they operate and whether this is likely to offer commercial fit opportunities for you or threats;
- industry- and client-specific issues that may represent commercial fit opportunities or threats;
- the reality of your relationship with each client.

You can do little to influence the reality of the current macro- or micro-economic positions: you can only respond to opportunities or threats. Based on the current perceptions of the client and your own, you can, however, decide whether the relationship:

- is as successful today as it can be for the foreseeable future;
- can be improved if necessary and if so to what extent;
- should be treated as a strategically important account;
- should be deemed a long-term development opportunity;
- should be managed on a 'respond when asked' basis.

The results will help you to define the characteristics of a 'perfect' client so that you can assess new business opportunities most effectively. In business development as in many areas of business it is not what you decide to do that adds greatest value but what you decide *not* to do: in this case, which opportunities you will not pursue and which client relationships to downgrade or drop and why.

In Chapter 2 we look in more detail at how to define your 'perfect' client and the benefits to you of doing so.

In a perfect world ...

02

In theory, there are numerous potential clients with whom you could work. Sadly, experience indicates that by no means all of them will be clients with whom you can be truly successful. Indeed, it is a rule of thumb among professional sales people that around a third of the clients on their database or rolodex are at best non-profitable. That leaves aside firms with whom, for whatever reason, they have not made contact even though they may form part of the 'territory'.

Most sales people maintain those 'poor' relationships because they feel that any revenue must be good revenue and that all revenue is the same. Neither belief is accurate. In fact, the time spent with those 'poor' clients almost always detracts from the development of opportunities that have far greater potential. To chase revenue is a myopic, tactical approach that will often lead you down a blind alley and limit your ability to develop your business to best effect.

The real issue is how to identify not simply those organizations where there may be a commercial fit but those where there is also a cultural fit and where your strengths can either eliminate a possible weakness or enable the leveraging of one or more strengths on the client side. At this point we enter the world of strategic business development. Strategic business development represents the 'operational art' of building your business. It links the day-to-day tactics of delivery for current clients, prospecting for new ones and sifting those new prospects to find those that can become new clients in the future to the strategic development of selected client relationships that become symbiotic and are recognized by both parties to be true business partnerships. Done well, it ensures that your business pipeline is always flowing and that you maximize the amount of time spent with clients where you are able to be most successful. You will be able to delight each of those clients (because you know exactly what outcomes they seek and what drives them at a deep emotional level) to the extent that they become great providers of onward referrals. 'Like refers like', so the better the client who refers you, the more likely it is that the referral will be of high quality.

We have already explored in outline the macro-economic context in which you and your clients/potential clients operate. The benefit of that broad understanding is to ensure that you can set realistic expectations for your clients' business and hence for your own. It helps to avoid both undue pessimism and over-confidence/complacency. When set against what you believe to be your strengths in your field, it also helps to identify the areas in which you may be able to find a commercial fit with certain types of client. That in turn begins to narrow down your universe of possible clients by excluding those that you probably cannot help either to fulfil a dream or to resolve a problem.

The 'perfect' client firm

In this chapter we explore how to identify the 'perfect' client firm for you so that you can begin both to filter and prioritize current clients and assess the real prospect of success with prospective clients. We also look at how those 'perfect' clients might see you and your firm.

Clearly, we need to look first at the universe of 'possible' clients for you, recognizing that you cannot practically work with any and all of them. Indeed it is arguable that to refine the range of clients with whom you seek to work to as narrow and focused a selection as possible helps you to become recognized as an expert in your chosen field and hence to win more of the available business in that sector. Your initial selection criteria will include broad categories such as:

- *Geography:* where can you realistically access and serve clients?
- *Size:* how large a client firm can you realistically serve given your resources and field of work?
- *Field of operation:* in what field would a good client firm be likely to work?

In terms of geography, the key word here is 'realistic'. If yours is a small consulting firm with 10 employees based in London, you could of course work with clients anywhere in the UK or indeed anywhere in the world. However, at some point, logistics begin to impact. The further you have to travel to meet key players at the client firm, the harder it will be to maintain relationships and the more it will cost you to do so both in time and money. That cost must in some way be passed on to the client and it will be rare that the price a client is willing to pay for a given service is completely elastic; at some point the client will say 'Enough!' It will be logistically easier for you to win and deliver work with clients based inside the M25. If you were to seek to work with clients based overseas, there may be issues over visa applications, work permits, etc. Those same issues may be less prominent in the case of a much larger firm that is itself a multinational.

The size of a client firm (whether measured in turnover or number of employees) need not be a barrier, although it is an obvious selection factor. However, it is often easier for a small professional services firm to win work and build excellent relationships within very large client firms than it is for a large professional service firm to work with a small client organization. My own firm, for example, with only a handful of associates, has won work with one of the Big Four accountancy firms, with several international law firms, with several global banks, and so on.

The field of operation of a client firm may not be important as a selection criterion. However, in many cases it will define the role that you can realistically expect to achieve at least in the early stages of the relationship. For example, my own firm has considerable experience of working with clients in the professional services world on a wide variety of issues. It has no experience of working with firms in the oil industry. Could we win work with a major oil company and deliver it successfully? Yes; but the entry point to that firm would have to be very well-defined and almost certainly in a narrow field that had some linkage to our previous experience − for example operational management issues, leadership development or business systems. We would probably be more likely to win work initially within a division of the firm and in one country rather than globally and we would almost certainly gain entry to that firm via a strong and highly focused referral. We look at the power or referrals and how to generate good ones in Chapter 3 and in more detail in Chapter 9.

Remember, people buy what is in their mind rather than what is in yours. You therefore need to understand how the clients perceive you and your firm so that you can match the needs you identify to the role in which the client has already positioned you. Over time, you can develop and alter that role based on their direct experience of working with you. Without that direct experience it is hard to ensure your credibility in a role that is incongruent with the client's pre-existing perceptions.

If we can ensure that there is a good correlation between client perceptions and the role you seek, this in turn will help to move you up the 'business relationship ladder' with clients. At this point we are looking at the client firm rather than the individuals within it and their various roles in the client relationship. We look at this in more detail in Chapter 6.

How to begin?

The starting point is to list your current client firms and break them down into 'good' and 'poor' categories. I recommend using a spreadsheet to do this exercise because it will be easier to sort the client list. If you have no current clients, because you have only very recently started your own business for example, you can still carry out the summary exercise but it will of course be in the abstract as you project the kind of clients with which you wish to work. Once you have experience with real clients, you can and should repeat the process and reassess.

What makes a client firm 'good' or 'poor'? It is not necessarily an exact science but depends largely on how dealing with a client feels for you. There may be clients where the potential or actual revenue for you and for your firm is high, but the individuals with whom you must deal are difficult, are focused on price rather than the contribution you can make to their business or simply don't share your values or those of your firm.

You may be forced to deal with them but it is likely that these relationships will prove to be sponges of time and energy and may well also be low on profit. Low profitability of a client relationship is often a signal that the relationship is in some way broken or that the client has you positioned in their mind in an incorrect role. It may also be that they are simply a price buyer with no interest in a value-adding relationship. If that is indeed the case, it may well be best to walk away from the business or, if possible, to hand these clients to a colleague who feels able to get on with them effectively. (Better to pass on to a colleague a potential client with whom they may be able to succeed rather than lose the client completely – although it is only common sense to issue a clear and open health warning as to why you are doing so.) If that proves impracticable, you may need to extricate yourself gently from the relationship. I have had to do this only twice in the last 10 years. Although there was a short-term loss of revenue, the time that became available to seek and develop other opportunities more than made up for it within 12 months.

The first cut

An initial assessment of existing client firms could look like Table 2.1.

TABLE 2.1   Initial assessment

Client name	Projected revenue next year	Potential profit level	Is this client a 'winner' of the future in its field?	Is there a good cultural/ personal/ commercial fit?	Summary rating (Good, Mediocre, Poor)

You can add in other factors as you wish. However, the more complex you make the assessment, the harder it becomes to decide whether a given client is 'good' or 'poor' for you. You might decide to drop the 'Projected revenue' column in favour of a subjective 'Can we win?' type of question. To repeat: this is not intended as a mathematically exact exercise but as a way to filter existing clients so that we can then define more closely and objectively what factors go to make a 'good' and indeed a 'poor' client in general terms. The benefit is that we can then define what an *ideal* client looks like so that we can focus future business development efforts where it seems most likely that we can win.

'Win' in this context is not simply gaining a new assignment but gaining it with a client where you can begin to build a long-term relationship that enables you to become a critical contributor to their business and hence be recognized as a true business partner. In other words, this is a relationship where both you and the client can feel that you are winners because you both gain from the relationship. The benefit of that partnership is to lock out both external and internal competitors within the client firm and to minimize price as an issue for you to expand your business with that client.

The second iteration

Having built your initial client list and decided which are 'good' or 'poor' in your eyes, the next step is to sort the spreadsheet, and group the clients in each category. Next, create two additional workbooks in the same spreadsheet: one for 'good' clients, one for 'poor'. Copy the relevant client names into the first column of each workbook, leaving the top row blank.

Looking first at the 'good' clients, now list across the first row, starting in the second column, all of the factors that, for you, make these clients 'good'. I recommend that you exclude measures such as turnover but focus instead on issues such as:

- cultural fit;
- personal liking and trust between you and key individuals at the client firm;
- clear opportunity to add value to the client's business;
- whether, in your view, the client will become or will remain a 'winner' in its field, etc.

To populate the list of factors fully, the question to ask yourself is: 'In light of my experience to date with each of my clients, what factors appear to me to be most important in defining a "perfect" client firm (recognizing that such a client may not in fact exist)?' The factors that you come up with at this stage will be in addition to those you used in your initial 'first cut' selection.

This is very much a 'player's choice' exercise. I suggest you add 'Profitability' as a final item (or at least 'Potential profitability') because, no matter how positive the relationship may be it is of no business value to you unless it is now or can become profitable for you. It otherwise represents what I call 'profitless prosperity' where you may see great turnover but make no money. No matter how 'strategically important' such a client may be for you, even if only in a negative sense by locking out a competitor, you must at some point ask why you allocate resource to a relationship that makes no money for you and for your firm.

The next step is to carry out the same exercise for clients that show up on your 'poor' workbook, to identify the factors that make these clients 'poor' in your eyes.

Having populated the top row of your two workbooks with the factors that identify 'good' or 'poor' clients in general terms, now run across the row for each client and add an X or a check mark in the cells to indicate that a given factor applies to that client. Not all factors will apply to all clients.

Each entry should be able to pass the 'devil's advocate' test. In other words, to ensure that you are being objective you should feel able to explain the entries on your workbook to a metaphorical (or actual) sceptical colleague. Check that your initial 'gut feel' about whether the client is either 'good' or 'poor' appears correct when you look at the number of relevant factors that show up. An example of one of your workbooks might look like Table 2.2.

TABLE 2.2   'Good' clients

Client name	Good cultural match with me/my firm	Strong personal relationship with one or more key people	We can make a clear contribution to their business	Likely to be one of tomorrow's winners in its field	Budget does not appear constrained	Strong profit potential
Mega Ltd	X		X		X	X
Tiny Ltd	X	X	X		X	
Medsize Ltd		X		X		X
XYZ Ltd		X	X		X	X

In this example, you might want to reassess whether Medsize Ltd is indeed a 'good' client, given that there is not a good cultural fit between you/your firm and them. It is also unclear that you can make a good contribution to their business. While you may be able to win some business from that firm in the short term, it seems unlikely on this basis that there is potential for a long-term relationship. That may be all the more important as they also seem unlikely to be one of the 'winners of tomorrow' in their field.

You can now identify what appear to be your current 'best' client firms, based on how many factors they check. There should be a close correlation with most of the factors that defined a 'perfect' client firm for you. Add in, where they are not already covered, the *reverse* of the factors that seem to be common to most of your 'poor' clients. For example, if one of your most common negative factors was an inability as a firm to take decisions, the positive version of that could be 'Decisive culture'. This will deliver a complete list of all the factors that, for you, define a 'perfect' client firm including those factors that predominate among your existing clients.

The 'perfect client firm' score-sheet

You can now develop your own 'perfect client firm' score-sheet, based on the combination of factors you have brought out. This can be used to assess new potential clients to determine your probability of long-term success and also to review existing relationships.

Complete one score-sheet for each client and one following each initial meeting with a prospective client. The score-sheet should be reviewed following each subsequent meeting until you actually win an assignment. It should be reviewed again after the assignment has been completed and at any major milestone. I recommend such a review at least twice a year as you move into 'relationship maintenance' mode. The reason is simply that things change. The senior director who was your initial sponsor may retire or move to a new firm; the client firm may find itself bought out by a competitor, etc. Change is the only constant in business and your assessment must stay abreast of it.

Build a table or spreadsheet along the lines Table 2.3, using your own list of positive selection factors.

The greater the number of factors you try to assess, the harder it will be to make objective judgements. I recommend not more than about 10 factors, and to stick to around seven or eight if possible: it will make the assessment simpler, even if it is less granular. Weight the maximum scores to reflect the relative importance of each factor in your eyes. Keep it simple, however.

This 'Perfect client score-sheet' (Table 2.3) brings together the different views that you have previously created at the individual client level. The benefit is to ensure that you are able to take an objective view of each client so that you can focus on those where the overall 'fit' seems best for you.

TABLE 2.3   'Perfect client' score-sheet example

Factor	Maximum score	My rating	Percentage score
Good cultural fit with me and my firm.	10		
Strong personal relationship with one or more key players.	5		
Identifiable commercial fit, ie I can see how we can add value to their business in general.	10		
I can see a specific opportunity to solve a problem or enable a key player to fulfil a dream.	10		
There seems to be budget available right now.	10		
I can identify at least some competitors and see how to differentiate my offering.	5		
Total	50		

When it comes to assessing a potential client or reviewing an existing relationship, it is obviously important to be honest and realistic in your scores. You are after all kidding nobody but yourself and there is no 'right' answer. In assessing the result, focus on the percentage score column. If any score is at 70 per cent or less, that should set off an alarm bell. If the total percentage is 70 or less, you will almost certainly need to develop an action plan to increase that score before you can become reasonably certain that this is a client where you have a good chance of success long term.

If any score is at or below 50 per cent and there is not an immediately obvious action that can be taken to raise it significantly, the alarm bell should be deafening. If the total score is 50 per cent or less, it is probably not worth pursuing the opportunity unless you *must* do so for external reasons (which may be as simple as you have been ordered to do so by someone senior enough to make such a demand and make it stick regardless of logic). Management by entrenchment can be hard to handle!

How does the client see you?

Having assessed what a 'perfect' client looks like for you, it is equally important to look at how such a client might perceive you and your firm. The benefit is to minimize the possibility of a mismatch between where you believe you can see a 'fit' with the client and what they have in mind. If that were to occur, it will prove hard to develop the relationship and to win business. The word 'perceive' is important. Perceptions may not be factually correct. However, once formed they are hard to alter to the extent that they can become reality for the person who holds them.

Perceptions are formed very rapidly; often within a matter of seconds in an initial meeting. Once a perception is formed, there is a tendency to look for factors that reinforce it and to discount factors that challenge it. We explore the issue of perceptions in more detail in Chapter 6 in relation to the development of your relationship with the individual client. At this point, we are simply trying to understand how a client might position you and your firm so that, when you set up a meeting, the role that you offer does not create dissonance with the client.

In other words, the client will already have you in some kind of 'box' in their mind's eye when you first meet them. To try to position yourself too far outside that box will usually cause friction until the client gains practical experience of working with you and can accept you in a different or broader role. That 'boxing' can, therefore, be changed but usually it takes time and is the result of several incremental steps. You can also alter that pre-existing positioning in a number of ways as you develop your own branding, which includes positioning yourself as an expert. We look at this in Chapters 3 and 4.

There are two overlapping elements to this exercise: how existing clients see you and how a potential 'perfect' client (with whom you have not yet engaged) might reasonably be expected to see you. With potential clients, you will be looking at firms that 'look as though' there may be a reasonable fit for you at a commercial level – you can see a problem that this kind of organization might well experience and an opportunity for you to resolve that problem. The firm would of course also meet the basic selection criteria in terms of size, location and field of operation.

For example, I have done quite a lot of work over the last 10 years with law firms both in the UK and elsewhere. Changes in the regulatory environment for lawyers in the UK combined with difficult market conditions may indicate that, while very large, global or multinational firms may be able to continue very much as they have over the last two or three decades, firms outside that 'magic circle' will face a need to consolidate by way of merger or takeover unless they can grow their practices organically and quite strongly.

In my experience, mergers (in whatever field) usually give rise to organizational change issues and unless these are handled well the planned cost savings and profit increases are rarely achieved. The only way to grow a practice, in my view, is to focus on the development of excellent client relationships rather than pure legal expertise. I have come across few lawyers who know how to do either of these things effectively. I have a successful track record in both areas. I can therefore identify two opportunities for me to help medium-sized law firms in the UK to do well in tough conditions. I can identify more than 30 firms that meet the basic selection criteria. The next step would be to filter these and then assess how each of them might see me and my firm so that I can work out how best to approach them.

Existing clients

In the case of existing clients, there is no substitute for asking questions directly of the client to find out what they feel. Those questions should be open (ie not capable of a simple 'yes/no' answer) and be non-confrontational. The aim is to gather information, not put the client on the defensive or damage the relationship. Questions to be asked (in your own words, of course) could include:

- What do you feel about our industry and our position in it?
- On a scale of 1 to 5 where 1 = commodity supplier and 5 = valued business partner, at what level do you feel our relationship with your firm lies today and why?
- If it is less than 5, what could we do to move up that scale?
- On a 1 to 5 scale, where 5 is high, how do you rate the fit for our services in your business and where do you see the best opportunities for us to work together in future?
- How do you feel that your clients experience the value of the services we provide to you?
- How does working with us feel for you? What would you like to change?
- If there was one thing that, assuming no constraints, we could do differently or better in our work with you, what would it be?
- What do you see as the most important strengths that we bring to our work with you?
- How can we best leverage those strengths to enable you to capitalize on what you see as a strategic opportunity?
- Where could we be (or become) vulnerable in your view?

The nature, tone and depth of the answers you receive will tell you a lot about the strength of the relationship you have with this firm and with the individual in question.

Potential client firms

In looking at potential clients, and in particular those that may have a high percentage score on your 'perfect client' criteria, it can be somewhat more complex to assess your likely position in their eyes, because you lack concrete data. That means that you are working in the dusk, if not in the dark. However, you can still make a good attempt to assess the degree of likely fit in the eyes of the client and consider what factors may improve your position.

In the UK law firms example I mentioned above, I identified two specific opportunities to find a commercial fit with potential clients like this. I can now begin to drill down and gather more information to assess which firms should be the centre of my attention and how they might see me or a firm like mine. My starting point is to build a list of firms that meet my initial selection criteria:

- Solicitors (as opposed to barristers, who have previously worked under a somewhat different regulatory regime and with a different function in that they had the sole right to represent clients in court, unlike solicitors).
- Based in London or in a major provincial city such as Bristol or Manchester (ie with good road, rail and air transport links).
- Having at least 20 partners and 50 fee earners.
- Turnover of at least £25 million per annum.

There are over four dozen such firms in the UK that I can identify based on an annual report produced by *The Lawyer*, the weekly newspaper for the UK legal profession. Having identified the firms in question, I can then begin to look at each one individually.

I might choose to look first at firms based in London because they are likely to be located within walking distance of my own office. An initial meeting will therefore be easy and require limited travel time. Over half of the firms I have identified are London-based.

I can now begin to use the internet and back copies of the relevant trade press to answer questions like those below. A basic Google search will often bring up a surprising amount of information, as will detailed reading of the firm's own website. Where I can identify likely key players within the firm (for example the senior partner and the head of HR and/or of learning and development, or the partner responsible for marketing) I can then look at their profiles on LinkedIn®. If they do not have one, I know that they may not be using technology to best advantage, which offers another commercial fit opportunity. Questions I would ask myself as I search could include:

- Has this firm any known history of using a firm like mine?
- If so, who was it?
- What do I know (or what can I find out) about it?

- What was the project on which it worked?
- What sort of results were achieved?
- What does the firm say about itself on its own website?
- What does it say about its corporate values and behaviours?
- How does it seek to engage with its clients?
- Does what it says focus on its technical expertise or on the development of great relationships with clients?
- What kind of clients does this firm serve and what is its USP?
- In what areas does it work (geographic and field of operation)?
- Do I get a sense of who the people running the firm are and do I like what I see?
- Is it likely that there would be a good cultural fit as well as a commercial fit?
- Is it essentially optimistic in what it says about itself or does it feel as if it sees itself backed up against a wall?
- What does it say about its future and its plans?
- What challenges might this highlight?
- Is there a clear and meaningful, client-focused strategy in its marketing documents, on the website or in other reports?
- What is it? Does it reinforce a commercial fit?
- What has been the trend in its turnover and profitability over the last two to three years?
- Do the numbers tally with what the firm says about itself?

Based on the answers to these and similar questions, I can then develop a score-sheet for each firm that will help me to identify both specific commercial fit opportunities and how the firm might perceive me and my firm if I were to approach them. The factors that you use will of course be your own selection based on what you feel is most relevant to you and the type of clients you prefer to work with.

This sounds like a lengthy process. However, in my experience, it need take probably not more than 30–45 minutes to bring together enough information on a given firm for your needs. Once again, you are looking for indicators, not an exhaustive and mathematically exact set of data. This is time well spent because it may save you considerable wasted effort later on in setting up meetings and having conversations where you cannot in fact be successful. That score-sheet might look like Table 2.4.

Once again you can assess the scores on the basis outlined above. If any score is 70 per cent or less, it should sound an alarm. If any score is 50 per cent or less you need to have an action plan to raise it rapidly. If the total score is 50 per cent or less it is probably best to look elsewhere.

TABLE 2.4 Potential client score-sheet example (UK law firm)

Factor	Maximum score	My perception rating	Percentage score
Identifiable commercial fit.	10		
Past experience in using external firms.	5		
Am I likely to be credible in delivering a solution to their commercial need?	10		
Does it seem likely that there is a good cultural fit?	10		
Where are they on a 'purgatory to paradise' spectrum (where purgatory = 1 and paradise = 10)?	10		
Do they appear to want help?	5		
Total	50		

I mentioned that I use this type of score-sheet to assess how the potential client firm might perceive me and my firm if I were to approach them. By 'approach them' I do not mean a completely cold call. In the professional services world, that is rarely successful. What I have in mind is further digging to find out if it may be possible to gain a referral or introduction to the firm. That may be from within my own network or via an online network such as LinkedIn®. If that is not possible, the next question would be whether I could engineer a meeting with somebody from the firm at, say, a conference or seminar. If that proves not to be possible, I could consider how to leverage my position as a recognized expert in a particular field that I believe to be relevant to that firm.

For example, I have spoken at a number of seminars on issues to do with practice growth and business development. I have a certain amount of 'collateral' (articles and other material that I have written) on that topic. I could certainly contact the firm and ask if there is a specific person responsible for the firm's marketing and business development (there often is, although it may be a fairly junior person). If it is indeed someone junior in the firm's hierarchy, that need not be a problem. In fact it may be easier to secure an initial meeting with someone at a more junior level at which you can begin to 'map' the firm in far greater detail. At any stage that mapping exercise may indicate that you should proceed no further, thus avoiding wasted time and effort.

Once I have that name, it is fairly easy to send a copy of a relevant article with a short covering letter outlining why I feel it may be of interest and suggesting a short conversation on the back of it. It is not an ideal way to gain access to a client firm but in my experience it is successful more often than not. At least one can then begin to gain concrete information that will confirm whether the firm is one where the fit (commercial and personal) is sufficiently good to warrant more work.

We explore the ideas of 'target acquisition' (ie identifying potential clients and ways to approach them – or helping them to find and approach you) and of linking the value that you deliver to results that are relevant to the client in more detail in Chapters 3 and 4.

Locating your perfect clients

03

So far we have looked at the context in which you and your clients operate, what constitutes a good – or even a 'perfect' – client for you and how such a client may perceive you and your firm. The benefit is to help you to focus on opportunities where you can be successful. Your success will of course entail helping the client to be successful in their terms by using one or more of your particular strengths to enable the client to resolve a felt problem or to fulfil a desire or dream.

It is now time to look at how to find potential new clients. This is only one part of your business development strategy, not its sole focus as many professionals seem to believe. It is at least as important to maximize the amount of business that you win from existing clients and its profitability: it takes far less time and effort to win business from a client with whom you have an existing relationship than to identify and win business from a new client. Indeed there are only three ways to build the bottom line of your business:

1 Find new clients and win business from them.

2 Win more business from existing clients (either by winning more pieces of work or increasing the value/profitability of each piece of work, or both).

3 Increase the profit margin of your business from all sources, whether by increasing prices, reducing cost or outsourcing non-core work to lower cost locations.

All of these things can and should be done in parallel.

Over time the mix of additional business from existing clients and new business from new clients will change as will (in all probability) the profitability of each piece of business, either because your fee rate rises or because your delivery becomes more efficient and cost is thus reduced. In the early stages of building a practice most of your effort will necessarily be focused on developing new clients and winning new business. Subsequently, you will be able to develop those relationships to deliver additional business. However, it is a mistake to focus all of your attention on cultivating existing clients: it tends to lead to complacency on both sides. Realistically, you should expect to lose a proportion of your client base each year. (Individuals who have acted as your sponsor in a client firm retire or move on, firms merge or are acquired, clients' needs change so that there is no longer a commercial fit for you, etc.) That business will need to be replaced in addition to any overall growth you wish to achieve. The search for new clients will always be with us.

In addition to finding new clients, we will also look at ways to expand your surface area with an existing client firm. For example, my own firm had worked with the investment management arm of a major bank for some time. We were then able to expand our involvement into the custody and administration arm of the same firm, which operates as a separate division and almost as if it were a completely separate company. That opportunity came by way of an internal referral, which was carefully engineered (something we explore in Chapter 9).

There are two aspects to what I have called 'target acquisition' in this context. The first is taking steps to locate, pre-qualify, approach, re-qualify and then begin to develop a relationship that allows you to work with a new client (in other words, looking outwards through the sights of your 'business sniper rifle'). The second is ensuring that you are visible to suitable potential clients so that they are able to find you and initiate contact with you. At that point you will still need to go through the qualification process and gather information to identify the necessary 'fit' at both a commercial and cultural level before you can move forward. However, the client has been able to pre-select (pre-qualify) themselves by expressing an interest in you and your firm. They have metaphorically put up a hand to indicate interest in an initial conversation. The benefits are obvious.

Both approaches will be necessary in the vast majority of professional services businesses. The mix will vary depending on factors such as how long your business has been established (more sniper-like activity is likely to be needed in the early days of a new firm) and personal temperament (some people prefer the thrill of the chase rather than the delivery of solutions).

Cultural fit – why it matters

The term 'cultural fit' has come up several times and will no doubt appear again. It is important because, in my experience, it is one of the key factors in the success or failure of any business relationship.

As an example of a failure to identify an aspect of cultural fit and its impact on winning business, I met at a conference some years ago the newly-appointed HR director of an IT business. The company was only about six or seven years old but had grown very rapidly to an annual turnover of around £80 million. This was due largely to the drive and hands-on leadership of the chief executive and owner of the business.

He had begun to experience some health problems and wished to spend more time sailing in the Mediterranean. He had two issues: 1) ensuring that the management team could assume full responsibility for running the business and continuing its growth, with a view to an eventual management buy-out or trade sale, and 2) how he himself could best make a transition from hands-on and active involvement in the business to being informed of what was going on, rather than being in direct control. The new HRD told me that this man had a very strong sense of business ethics and was keen to do the best for the people in the business, most of whom had been with him for several years. I did not clarify what she meant by the term 'strong sense of business ethics'; I assumed that she meant 'doing the right thing' in the way the business was run. As ever, assumption is the mother of error.

On the face of it, however, it was a case of so far, so good. There was a clear commercial fit. I could identify two opportunities for me to help the chief executive to resolve a problem and indeed to fulfil a dream. I believed that my experience was of direct relevance and it appeared to be an interesting opportunity to work with a dynamic individual and in all probability with a high calibre team in a rapidly growing business.

During the first few minutes of my initial meeting with the chief executive, it became clear that he was a convinced pacifist and strongly anti smoking and alcohol. He made a point of telling me that he had refused a number of lucrative contracts with the Ministry of Defence and with various tobacco and drinks companies on the grounds that it went against his business ethics. I said that we should probably end the meeting at that point as it seemed unlikely that we could work together effectively, given that I was a former Army officer who enjoyed a glass of wine and even an occasional cigar.

The sniper rifle approach

We have looked at an approach to identify the factors that define a 'perfect' client for you. These need not be fixed for all time. They may well develop over time or even change quite radically if, for example, your firm gains an additional capability or opens an additional office in another city or country. We know that it is not practicable for you to work with every possible client so your sights need to zero in on opportunities where the probability of success appears to be high.

Note the word choice: 'probability' rather than 'chance'. All the preparation that we are looking at is designed to minimize if not eliminate chance or luck as a factor in winning business and ensuring that the business is profitable for you. It may seem to be dull and unglamorous but this sort of preparation will save you much wasted time and effort and enhance your results hugely while at the same time reducing the stress of feeling overwhelmed by too many choices.

The work already covered in the first two chapters gives a sound base from which to build. The next step is to begin actively to seek potential clients. There are several possible approaches:

1 Seek referrals or introductions from within your own network or via the networks of colleagues.
2 Be present in locations where potential clients are also likely to be present and ready to engage with selected individuals.
3 Formal networking.
4 Research followed by a direct approach.

1. Referrals and introductions

If it is possible to gain a referral to a new potential client, it can be extremely helpful because you avoid the friction of being an unknown trying to gain access to the firm and to individuals within it. By implication you borrow the pre-existing credibility of the person who makes the referral. I call this 'transitive property'.

For example, your friend Fred likes and trusts you. He also likes and trusts Alice who in turn likes and trusts Fred and respects his opinions. Alice is in a senior position at a bank and is about to embark on a major reorganization which is fraught with problems. Fred knows that you are an expert in organizational change. If Fred refers you to Alice and places you in the role of expert in organizational change, he lends you his credibility with Alice. That puts you several steps ahead in developing your own relationship with Alice and winning business with her. The referral will not dilute her relationship with Fred; indeed it may enhance it. (That of course assumes that you and Alice do not suffer what I think of as an 'oil and water' moment, otherwise known as visceral dislike and that you do not fail to live up to Alice's expectations.)

There is a distinction between a referral and an introduction. An introduction is essentially a social interaction with a business overtone: 'Alice, this is Stephen. He runs a consulting and executive coaching firm; used to be in the Army and spent 20 years in the City. Stephen, Alice runs the London office of ABC Bank; she's looking at a reorganization soon. Her son is thinking of going into the Army after university. Maybe you two might want to talk about that over coffee sometime?'

An introduction like that can be made by almost anyone and is often almost accidental. The 'credibility transference' may be quite low initially but it is a useful way to be helped to start a conversation from which you can develop your own credibility and adjust your perceived role in the eyes of the potential client (if that is what he or she proves to be). However, it does not necessarily set you up in the optimal role that will enable you to win business.

In the example above, Alice now has me mentally positioned in the role of 'potential career adviser to my son'. I may indeed be able to help him and would almost certainly be willing to do so. However, that is not the role I seek with Alice herself. If it proves to be appropriate (ie, if she passes my 'client qualification filter'), I would like to talk to her about possible opportunities to help her make a success of the reorganization she is contemplating. In most cases, the best outcome from an introduction like this will be a further meeting. The way in which you set up that meeting dictates its probability of success, and we look at that process in Chapter 7.

A referral, by contrast, is a specific and prepared introduction for business purposes. It links a known need of the potential client to a specific capability or expertise of yours and reinforces your personal credibility with the person making the referral. It makes a specific recommendation that you and the potential client should meet and outlines the goal of that meeting. The key is that you need to be able to explain, clearly and succinctly, to those individuals that you trust to make a referral exactly what you are looking for in terms of:

- the type of client (both at the firm and at the individual level) including size, geography and field of operation if appropriate;
- the role you seek in general terms with that type of client;
- the action you would like the person you are asking to make a referral to take.

We look in some detail at preparing a great referral in Chapter 9.

2. Being present in the same locations as potential clients

We look at this in some detail in the following section of this chapter as it is both a way in which you can actively seek new clients and a way in which to become visible to potential clients so that they are able to pre-qualify you and seek you out when they are ready to do so. However, think in terms of attendance at conferences, seminars and trade shows where you are likely to find potential clients that match closely the definition of your 'perfect' client, which we examined in Chapter 2.

For example, the weekly periodical for the legal profession, *The Lawyer*, organizes a number of conferences each year. If my 'perfect client' was a large law firm and specifically the senior partner in that firm, I might well consider attending *The Lawyer*'s annual Law Firm Strategy Conference, especially if strategy (or perhaps strategy implementation) were one of my own or my firm's areas of expertise and I could therefore identify at least one area of commercial fit with attendees.

3. Formal networking

Networking is an abused word. It conjures up the 'business card exchange fest' over breakfast where attendees make a formal 'elevator pitch' for 30 seconds and success is measured by the number of new business cards obtained. Done well, networking can be a great way to build your business over time and has multiple benefits. It does require time, planning and focused effort, however. In most cases, successful business development in a professional services context will require at least some networking. We look at how to do it effectively and relatively painlessly even if you are by nature an introvert, later in this chapter.

4. Research followed by a direct approach

This is not the classic cold call approach such as one I experienced recently: 'Hello. I need to speak to a decision maker ...' to which the natural response is of course, 'Please leave your message at the click ...' as the telephone receiver is replaced. In this case the direct approach will be to:

- an identified individual who ...
- holds a position within a potential client firm that you have already decided has a close correlation to the factors that define a 'perfect' client for you and ...
- where you can identify at least one potential opportunity to articulate a 'commercial fit' for you to work with that firm ...
- that, if implemented, would provide a real and measurable benefit for the client.

Taken together, this all adds up to a legitimate reason for you to make a direct approach; it is not a cold call as such. How do you identify these factors? The simple answer is 'research' – which can be combined with industry knowledge where you have a specific field of expertise that is industry specific.

You already know what constitutes a good potential client. At the end of Chapter 2, I outlined an approach to identifying law firms that might be good candidates for me to approach on behalf of my own firm. A similar approach can be adopted in almost any other industry or profession. The critical issue is to be able to identify what comprises the target group so that you can then select from within it. It is, in my view, relatively easy to filter law firms based on size, turnover, etc because there is a fair amount of data available in the public domain. Anybody willing to spend around £3 can buy a copy of *The Lawyer* and see its annual report on the top 200 firms. A half-year subscription costing £40 allows access to its website and to quite detailed information on each firm. If you cannot filter information on a target group to identify those where there seems to be a good potential commercial fit, it may be easier to identify a different group. You are looking for firms and individuals where there is an identifiable problem and an opportunity for you to help them resolve that problem. It will otherwise prove hard to reach the relevant people and much of your marketing and sales effort will be wasted.

If your target audience comprises not firms or organizations but individuals (for example a private wealth manager or someone involved in executive recruitment), the research task is arguably more important. It is not necessarily harder. It is likely to be different and to require at least one additional step. The research task in this context is so important that many firms employ research specialists who are able to focus on it full time and have the necessary tenacity and attention to detail, and the ability to see possible connections.

Whether or not you use a research specialist, you will still need to go through the process of describing a 'perfect' client and the economic context in which you both operate. To the extent that you are able to identify specific individuals that you would like to do business with, it will be necessary to spend time on considering the best legitimate reason for you to make contact (the 'fit') and how to gain either a referral or an introduction if at all possible. The judicious use of social networking sites such as LinkedIn can help but it can be more effective to look for organizations or individuals you know or to whom you can gain introductions and who in turn can help you to get to those who act implicitly or explicitly as gatekeepers. We look in more detail at the use of social networks and developing your professional network later in this chapter.

Technology: a side note

The advent of the internet changed everything in terms of the availability of data and the vastly increased speed and reduced cost of that availability. It changed nothing in terms of the need to refine that data to make it useable. Similarly, great technology does not compensate for poor marketing and sales processes and/or people. If anything it raises the bar of excellence in these areas. Used well, however, good technology can enhance your sound marketing and sales processes and enable good people to perform better by streamlining aspects of their work.

By no means all firms need or will use effectively a dedicated CRM system. Indeed I can think of very few firms I have worked with that have implemented a good CRM system, done it well and used it effectively. That does not mean to say that such firms only rarely exist nor that it is impossible to 'do' CRM well. In my experience, the keys to success are simplicity both of system design and data structure, and ensuring that data capture is as automated as possible – and is a by-product of 'business as usual'.

If data input is a separate function or requires executives whose role is essentially client-facing to do it manually, there is a high probability that data will become out of date rapidly. That will surely mean that the CRM system falls into disuse and (eventually) individuals will build their own personal or local systems.

The choice of CRM system can be complex. In most cases it is possible to gain an effective 80 per cent solution that is relatively simple and low cost: few firms really need a full-scale Oracle® implementation or similar. For a small firm with a handful of employees, a lot can be achieved using basic Microsoft Outlook® or an Access® database. Both will need manual effort to maintain and in particular to undertake things like e-mail marketing campaigns. The use of a piece of software such as ACT® by Sage can help to automate some processes such as timed follow-ups and can keep track of e-mail and other communication to clients and prospective clients.

One of my clients is a firm that has fewer than 10 employees but a substantial overhead in automated e-mail-based marketing campaigns that have proven to be very successful. The owner of that business has a database of approximately 4,500 clients and prospective clients. He is evangelical about the benefits of Infusionsoft® (**www.infusionsoft.com**) as a way to automate much of his firm's client e-mail communication, and Highrise® (**www.highrisehq.com**) to keep track of all communication with clients by whatever means. They also use Highrise® as something akin to a workflow management tool. Neither requires significant investment in hardware or software and expenditure can be limited to a reasonable monthly outlay. The ceiling on the number of clients that can be managed using this kind of approach is significant – 30,000 in the case of Highrise® for example – and would cover the needs of very many businesses in the professional services field.

To reiterate, there are many systems and solutions available: those mentioned above are examples only. Many of the available 'enterprise' solutions probably represent overkill for the majority of small and medium-sized businesses.

Keep the system and the process of using it simple, design your processes on paper first and automate what you have designed step-by-step 'in little' before moving to a fully-fledged system. That way you can iron out bugs as you discover them and hence reduce risk. Always keep a back-up of your data before you change a system or move to a new one. Keep focused on what you *must* be able to do rather than what you (or a software salesman) might like and you are likely to end up with something that is effective and works well for your needs. A Rolls Royce solution may well be tempting, but a VW Golf equivalent will get you to your destination safely and in reasonable comfort at a far lower cost.

Being visible

So far we have focused on ways in which you can identify potential clients with whom you wish to explore opportunities for you to add value to their business or to them personally. The latter offers you a legitimate reason to make contact directly or (preferably) by way of an introduction or referral. In this section we explore how to become visible to prospective clients so that they are able to locate you as and when they are ready to do so.

In making contact with you, they will have pre-qualified themselves as having a potential 'fit' because you will be taking steps to ensure that you are visible in one or more clearly identifiable roles, which in turn suggest opportunities for a commercial fit between you and those potential clients who want (as well as need) the benefits that you can offer. The questions are therefore: what do you want to make visible to prospective clients, and how can you make it visible in a manner that is congruent with your chosen role and authentic for you?

We look at the 'What ...' question in Chapter 4. As to the 'How ...', the following section looks at:

1 Social networks and offline networking.
2 Positioning yourself as an expert.
3 The discrete use of PR.
4 Online search.
5 The importance of a list – and how to build one.

1. Social networks and offline networking

There are many social networks available and the number is increasing. Not all of them will be appropriate for you in a professional services context although you may want to be able to access some in person to locate and communicate with certain individuals. The benefit of social networks is that they allow you to be 'found' online – to become visible – and for people to find out something about you before making contact. It is akin to observing someone on the other side of a crowded room in order to assess whether you wish to go across and talk to them.

What you show to others online is therefore as important as what you show in real life; perhaps more so because once information is 'out' on the web, it is effectively visible for all time to those who know how to find it. Take care therefore that what you make generally available online is material that you would be happy for others outside your immediate friendship circle to see and that it is congruent with the role that you seek professionally.

Even if you restrict access to your personal data (your Facebook® page, for example) it may be that someone among your Facebook® friends has no such restrictions. If you appear and are 'tagged' in a photograph that appears on that person's Facebook® account, you are immediately identifiable. My step-daughter was surprised that her mother had seen certain (relatively innocuous) holiday photos that were on her 'friends only' Facebook® page. They also appeared on the 'open' page of a friend with tags identifying each person, including my step-daughter. I understand that it is possible to 'un-tag' yourself from all photographs on Facebook® but not everyone does so. In deciding whether to use any given social network, it is essential to think through your answers to a few questions:

- Is it relevant? (Do my clients use it? Would my 'perfect' client be likely to use it?)
- Is it appropriate to the role I seek with my clients and potential clients?
- Do I understand the security and privacy issues relating to this particular network?
- Do I have the time and resources to make effective use of this network? (There is little point in a Twitter account with only a handful of tweets, the most recent of which is several months old.)

Several social networks may seek to occupy similar space on the web; Xing and LinkedIn® for example both offer 'business networking'. However, they approach the topic differently and offer different functionality. These networks vary tremendously in size: Xing has around 11 million users and LinkedIn® over 100 million, for example.

To give an idea of the sheer volume of 'social networks' available world-wide, Wikipedia lists over 200 of them, excluding dating and 'adult' sites. In deciding how best to use social networks to enhance your visibility online, it is impractical and almost certainly inappropriate to develop a profile on all social networks. It will be far more effective to select a small number (probably not more than three or four) on which to focus.

In the professional services field in the western world, the following will likely serve you best: LinkedIn®, YouTube®, Twitter®, Facebook® and (perhaps) Second Life®. The following is by no means an exhaustive explanation of how to go about maximizing the value to you of each of these sites; that is beyond the scope of this book. The aim is to highlight key opportunities and caveats. For a deeper but still general (as opposed to technical) insight into social media, I recommend the book *Get up to Speed with Online Marketing* by Jon Reed, published by FT Prentice Hall.

A website

Before you begin, you should of course have an online presence in the form of a website. Most professional services firms will have one. Individuals setting up a new business will certainly need one: it is as essential as a business card used to be 20 years ago.

There are many ways to set up a website and it need not be technologically advanced to be extremely effective. Many web hosting companies (such as Fasthosts, One & One and Host Gator) offer website templates as part of their hosting service. All that you need to do is copy and paste in content that you have written and digital images from your own resources as required.

An excellent alternative is Wordpress (**www.wordpress.org**) which offers a robust and flexible platform free of charge, but with the option to add 'plug-ins' (think in terms of 'apps') that add functionality at a very reasonable cost (often free of charge).

If the creation of a website is not something about which you feel confident, outsource it. Some competent professionals can be found via Elance (**www.elance.com**). Elance is an online exchange where one can post a description of a job ('I need a website built') to which suitably qualified professionals can respond with an offer of a price to complete the work. The more detailed and specific the description of the job on which you seek bids, the less likely it is that there will be disappointment.

Elance provides reviews of work completed and ratings by users, rather in the manner that eBay carries ratings of sellers and Amazon carries ratings of suppliers. That online reputation is hard won and can be quickly lost so those with high ratings guard them jealously by doing good work at a very reasonable cost. Many are based in locations such as India or Russia, but language is rarely a barrier and you can gain the advantage of their low local cost base.

LinkedIn®

Of the various social networks, for those in the professional services field, LinkedIn® is almost an essential. It can be a source of new business, especially for consultants, project managers and independent professionals such as lawyers and accountants. It is also likely to be one of the first places that a prospective client will look to 'check you out' prior to a meeting.

The key to success with LinkedIn® is to have a full and up-to-date profile complete with a photograph of you and at least two recommendations; more if possible. The profile needs to give the reader a feel of 'who you are' as well as 'what you have done'. It should encourage that person to make contact with you to find out more. Many professionals find it hard to build an effective profile for themselves, not least because they find it hard to be open about their success ('Don't want to blow my own trumpet ...'). Of course if you are unwilling to blow your own trumpet, at least a little, nobody else will do it for you. The profile should make clear the benefits of working with you: more of this in Chapter 4 where we explore brand building and management. If the technical aspects of creating a profile and ensuring that it is as effective as possible appear daunting, it can also be outsourced. A friend and client of mine, Rob Kerner, is an expert on LinkedIn® and in building great LinkedIn® profiles based on a full CV and (in some cases) a phone call. His fee represents very good value, in my view. He can be contacted by e-mail at rob@corporatefixer.com.

In your early days of using LinkedIn® you can manage perfectly well without a Premium account, the main initial benefit of which is to be able to send an 'InMail' – the internal version of e-mail – to other members. It is likely, however, that you will soon want to move away from the 'free' version and sign up for a Premium account, which adds a number of features such as:

- Contact anyone on LinkedIn via InMail.
- Access expanded profiles of people outside your network.
- See more profiles with every search.
- Use of advanced search filters.
- Get the full list of Who's Viewed Your Profile.
- Manage your contacts and profiles more effectively.
- Get full name visibility for all third-degree connections.

Some people seem to define success on LinkedIn® in terms of the sheer number of connections they have. In my view, it is not the number but the quality of the connections that matters and whether you are able to manage them effectively. There is no point in having 800 connections if the last time that 700 of them heard from you was when you sent them a request to connect. We look at network building and maintenance later in this chapter.

LinkedIn® now offers the opportunity to advertise within LinkedIn® to a highly targeted audience that can be selected based on factors including job title, job function, industry, geography, company size, company name, seniority, age, gender or LinkedIn® group. In terms of cost to advertise, there are two alternative approaches: pay per click (PPC) or cost per 1,000 impressions (CPM). Most people choose PPC, which means that you pay when someone clicks on your advertisement. This payment method allows you to specify a bid – the maximum amount you're willing to pay for each click (for example, $3 per click) subject to a minimum of $2 per click. To learn more, visit **www.linkedin.com** and click the Advertising link on the navigation bar.

Google® pioneered this type of advertising approach with its AdWords programme. It is likely that most online social networks and search providers will in future follow this approach if they are not doing so already.

YouTube®

YouTube® is second only to the mighty Google® as an online search medium and is indeed now owned by Google®. The benefit to you of using YouTube® is that it allows you not only to be found online but to be literally seen online by way of short video appearances. These allow you to highlight specific areas of expertise. They can be designed specifically for your target audience – ie to interest those individuals that meet the criteria you determined earlier as defining your 'perfect client'.

Video is a powerful medium and can allow your personality to shine through as you talk about your topic. It can also be a double-edged sword: you can generate all kinds of unwanted perceptions just as easily as making a strong personal connection. Before you upload videos, it is advisable to create a few samples (they need only be a couple of minutes in length) and ask for feedback on them from friends and colleagues. It is critical to be perceived as 'being yourself' and delivering interesting insights in a relaxed and succinct manner. Talking to a camera need be no different to talking to a friend in your own home.

It may seem daunting to create videos, as well as costly. In fact the equipment needed can be minimal; just a basic video camera (even a 'Flip' type camera will do the job), a tripod on which to mount it and, ideally, a piece of editing software. I use Sony Movie Studio, but there are several other great programs available including Corel Video Studio Express and Adobe's Premiere Elements. All the basic equipment can be bought for less than £200. I would add an external microphone (and of course ensure that the camera is able to accept an external microphone connection). The cost need be no more than £20 or so and the sound quality of your video will be improved immensely. If and when necessary, you can invest in specialist lighting equipment, which also adds to the professional 'feel' of your production. There is a learning curve involved in working out how to use the camera and software, but you can learn to produce perfectly viable short video clips and post them to YouTube® in a morning.

Once you have videos posted on YouTube® it is advisable to place a link to the videos on your own website. You can of course also include the same link in any e-mail marketing messages you send to clients and prospective clients.

Twitter®

Twitter® is a micro-blogging site that allows users to post short messages of up to 140 characters in length. It represents the Haiku equivalent of online communication media. Whether you elect to use Twitter® or not will depend on the nature of your target audience and whether Twitter® is an 'authentic' medium for you in the role that you seek with clients. Part of that decision will be driven by the age of your audience. In its early days, most Twitter® users were aged below 30. It seems that most of their new users are now aged over 35. A similar phenomenon can be seen with Facebook® and a number of other social networks.

The key question is whether the people to whom you wish to be visible are likely to be users of Twitter®. If you have reason to believe that they are, it behoves you to become involved and decide how best to use it to your advantage professionally. As with your YouTube® videos, make sure that what you have to say is likely to be both interesting and relevant to your target audience. The 140 character limit on Twitter posts ensures brevity. It may also be helpful to have in mind the remark made by David Cameron before he became Prime Minister, in an unguarded moment on Radio 4's *Today* programme, to the effect that 'Too many Tweets makes a twat.'

Facebook®

Originally developed as a communication medium for US university students (and at that time available only to those with a US university e-mail address), Facebook® has become the most commonly used of all social networks. Indeed for many younger users it has all but replaced e-mail. My step-daughter maintains an e-mail account so that she can get in touch with older relations. It is also used for 'mundane' things such as job applications and in her case as an ad-hoc back-up of data such as university essays and lecture notes. Some firms now use an in-house equivalent of the Facebook® concept instead of e-mail.

Once you have a personal Facebook® account, you can create a 'business page' that may be linked to your personal account. Like other social networks, Facebook® is now offering targeted advertising opportunities akin to Google®'s Adwords. The aim is to develop a community around your business, with individuals encouraged to (in effect) make an introduction of you and your business to their Facebook 'friends' in several different ways.

Once again, your decision to use Facebook® for your business will depend largely on the nature of your target audience and the authenticity of Facebook® for you personally as well as for your business in the role that you seek for clients. I do not use Facebook® (as yet) because it does not 'feel' right for me and, more important, most of my existing clients tell me that they see it as something used by their teenage children as a social communication network and not as a credible business tool. That may change.

As with all social networks, it is important to understand the privacy and security aspects of the way you use Facebook® – essentially who can see what. The HR director of a large law firm told me that a promising prospective trainee was not hired after her holiday photos, showing some deeply inappropriate behaviour, were open for anyone to see on Facebook®.

Second Life®

When I first came across Second Life®, my initial reaction was that it appeared to be an alternative to daytime TV for the technically savvy with time on their hands.

Second Life® is a virtual world that users inhabit in the form of a virtual character or avatar. It has its own currency. As in the real world, purchases of all kinds can be made. In Second Life®, one uses virtual currency bought with real cash. That has allowed a small number of people to build significant real wealth by activities such as virtual property purchases and sales made in the virtual world with the virtual currency units subsequently translated back into real money. In addition, a number of businesses have created virtual replicas of their products and prototypes and displayed them in a Second Life® to gain feedback from customers from many different locations in the real world, far beyond their normal reach.

I find it hard to see how a presence within Second Life® may be appropriate to my own clients and potential clients and indeed to most professional services firms. I am not sure that it offers a valuable way to build a business in the real world – at least for the time being. That is of course purely a personal view.

Offline network building

Despite the advent of social networks, the need for effective network building and maintenance offline is at least as important now as it has been in the past.

Effective network building is highly targeted and linked directly to a rigorous process to nurture the network as it is built. It is not about sheer numbers of names in your contact list or connections on LinkedIn®, nor is it about attending innumerable breakfasts organized by one of the firms whose business is organizing general business networking meetings. These are, in my experience, useless for practical purposes in the professional services context. However, they can work well in other business contexts. If you can identify networking meetings that are focused on your target client base, that may be productive: by all means give these a try but consider carefully how effective the meetings are in achieving the specific results you seek before signing up for an extended membership contract. You have already defined a 'perfect' client for you including the likely commercial fit opportunities. In order to build your professional network you will be seeking people who work for firms that meet your selection criteria. You will also have a good idea of what a good client would look like as an individual. Your networking should obviously focus on that kind of person where possible. There are four key elements in your approach:

1 knowing where your 'perfect' clients are likely to be found;
2 ensuring that you are able to be present there too and positively visible;
3 preparing prior to the event; and
4 nurturing the relationship once you have established initial contact.

There are two absolute requirements for effective network building and nurturing. The first is a 'giving' mind-set. It is far more effective to think 'What can I give to this person?' or 'How could I help them?' than to consider what you might gain. This becomes easier if you have available a variety of marketing collateral, such as we consider in Chapter 4. The second is being interested as opposed to interesting (in other words, asking questions rather than making statements).

In terms of where your clients are to be found, think of seminars, conferences and trade shows. In my earlier example, if my 'perfect' client is the senior partner of a medium-sized law firm and the likely commercial fit is around strategy implementation or organizational change, I will be looking for conferences or seminars on strategy and/or organizational change, probably organized by one or other of the legal periodicals or by the Law Society.

Having identified one or more possible opportunities, I will either apply to attend as a delegate or contact the organizers about the possibility of being a speaker at one of the sessions. That suggestion is more likely to be accepted if I am already positioned as an expert in the relevant field (something we explore in the next section of this chapter).

If that is not possible, I would prepare prior to the event by reviewing the list of attendees (which the organizers will usually provide on request, at least in the form of a list of firms attending if not with the names of individuals). Based on your previous research you can focus on those firms with which you wish to make contact and if possible identify the relevant person. I would also review the list of topics to be covered during the seminar or conference and research the speakers.

Based on that information, I would think about specific issues that appear relevant to the audience and that link to my specific 'commercial fit' opportunity, and then consider what might be effective lines of questioning to a speaker following a session. The benefit of asking good questions following a conference or seminar session is to become immediately visible to those attending and to indicate that you have knowledge of the subject matter and interesting insights. That can then encourage post-session conversations with other attendees. It also starts a process of 'becoming known on the circuit', which in turn makes it easier to start conversations with individuals you may have seen at previous events.

During the breaks between seminar sessions, by all means take refreshments, etc as required but make use of opportunities to open conversations, especially if you are able to identify someone you have previously decided might be a good client. As ever, ensure that your conversation opening is authentic for you and so far as possible follows the line of 'seriousness of purpose but levity of approach'. It may help to prepare a few opening questions in advance. (In Chapter 4 we look at how you answer one of the three killer questions: 'What do you do?' which is likely to come up early in any such conversation.)

By way of closing a conversation, you can ask for a business card, offer a piece of your marketing collateral (which automatically secures 'permission' to make at least one further contact by e-mail or post) or suggest a further informal meeting to expand on the current conversation. Which approach is appropriate will usually be clear at the time. However, where you feel that there is merit in further contact, it will usually be up to you to initiate it. If you do not feel that further contact will be helpful to you or to the individual, do not force it; it will almost certainly prove to be a waste of time for both of you. If further contact is requested, but you cannot see value for both of you, by all means decline gently. Many average sales people willingly add another card to the rolodex and 'meet to meet'. Very few good sales people do so because they recognize it is simply not a good use of time.

Before attending any event at which potential clients are likely to be present, it pays to think about what results you would like to achieve. That will usually be along the lines 'Meet Fred Smith from MegaFirm' or, 'Meet somebody from MegaFirm who might be able to help me gain access to Fred Smith.' You will be more likely to focus on securing those opportunities if you have pre-planned them and hence be more likely to succeed.

Trade shows are somewhat harder when it comes to preparation. You can and should take a look at the list of exhibitors and, if possible, attendees who have signed up pre-event. In the case of attendees it is unlikely that you will be given the names of individuals but a list of firms attending is quite likely to be available – certainly to possible exhibitors. If you feel able to approach the organizer as a possible exhibitor, you will of course gain the information you seek. However, be prepared to receive an unstoppable rush of marketing material by post and e-mail for some years, even if you do not in fact exhibit at the event.

Before you attend a trade show make sure that you know in your own mind why you are there and how you will judge your success after the event. 'Just getting a feel of what's new in the XYZ industry' may sound woolly, but is in fact a perfectly good reason to attend a trade show; it should allow you to see additional commercial fit opportunities with existing clients. To be successful in any field, you probably need to know as much about the business of your clients as they do. You will find a downloadable report on preparing to attend events such as conferences and trade shows on the website associated with this book: **www.professionalsbusinessdevelopment.com**.

Whether you encounter an individual at a conference, seminar, trade show or via a social network, you will almost certainly at some point wish to have a conversation with them and ideally one-to-one. While you may well need to establish your initial contact online or by e-mail, you are not, in my view, communicating effectively by using that medium. E-mail is really about passing information. It takes verbal interaction (by phone, videoconference or face-to-face) to communicate. The purpose of your initial networking contact is to set up an opportunity for a conversation. We look at how to plan and run such conversations most effectively in Chapter 7.

As you work to extend your network, you will also need to nurture it. That requires the investment of some time. However, if it is well planned the nurturing process can be done effectively without taking over your life. The key to success is an appropriate frequency of relevant and interesting communication, delivered in a manner that is appropriate for the client and authentic for you. This needs to be planned, prepared and delivered so far as possible automatically.

First, choose your communication medium. Although e-mail is not in my view a good tool for real communication (which I believe requires a verbal exchange and is best done face-to-face), it is highly effective for 'keeping in touch' and can be automated fairly easily. Hard-copy letters have similar characteristics to e-mail but are now far more powerful because they are relatively less used nowadays. Telephone calls (or Skype, etc) can be scheduled automatically and require longer to execute, although they are far more powerful than e-mail in building your relationship with the individual to whom you are speaking. Face-to-face meetings are yet more powerful but require longer planning and longer to achieve as they will usually involve at least some travel time.

Second, think about what you want to say. There is no point in communicating if you have nothing more interesting to say than 'Hi. How are you?' Never make contact with a client unless you are either trying to set up a meeting, in which case you will need a viable reason for them to say 'Yes' – ie some tangible benefit to them – or giving them something that is of interest and relevant to them. It may be a piece of information. It may be a link to a new video you have posted on YouTube® (so long as it is relevant to them). It may be information about a new product or service (ditto).

The choice of medium will be influenced by what you have to communicate. E-mail is excellent for routine items such as a 'tip of the week' (if you provide one to clients) and/or providing a link to a new YouTube® video, for example. Hard-copy letters will normally be seen as more personal, especially if you 'top and tail' them by hand (ie hand-write the salutation and signature block, with the rest of the letter in typescript). That was a commonly used approach to personalize a 'form letter' in the days before the advent of the internet and e-mail. If you need to have a conversation with the client, it has to be by phone, video conference or face-to-face. As a friend of mine puts it, 'Interaction means in-da-room' (which he delivers in an Italian accent with a strong overlay of Bronx).

Third, think about how often you need to be in touch with a given client to keep the relationship warm. As a rule of thumb I feel that I need to be in touch with someone in some way or another at least once each quarter to remain on their Christmas card list. If I hope to have a stronger relationship than that it had better be more like once a month. With a client for whom I have recently completed a piece of work, it will be more like weekly for at least four to six weeks, after which it will drop to fortnightly and then monthly. Some of those communications will be meetings or phone calls. There has to be a purpose for each, however; I always seek to meet for a reason over and above 'just to catch up' unless the meeting really is social, in which case I will say so. The client will tell me if he or she has other ideas.

I use a spreadsheet to keep track of which clients fall into which contact category. For several years I used MS Outlook™ to manage my e-mail contacts and schedule 'mass' communications. I now prefer an auto-responder that can be set up to automate the process. A basic auto-responder would be something like Mailchimp® which allows you to send e-mails automatically to up to 500 contacts free of charge. Others include AWeber® and Constant Contact®. Each has slightly different features and price structures but does a similar job.

Each week, I set aside time to get in touch with clients, based on the list in my spreadsheet. If the time is not scheduled it is far too easy to let the moment slip by and it becomes hard to catch up, with the result that you drop out of the client's short-term memory due to lack of contact or, worse, give the perception that you no longer care about them.

I can use this largely manual approach because the numbers are not large enough to cause a problem. If I allowed them to become so, it would be a signal that I must either hire another person or retrench my business. I also use spare time such as travel between meetings to make phone calls or type e-mails: micro-blasts of communication that can be highly effective. Each e-mail or call is planned, however briefly, in much the same way as I plan a meeting.

It is vital to ensure that your client data is kept fully up to date and 'cleaned' periodically. An American who is widely acknowledged as a master of network building, Keith Ferrazzi, in his book *Never Eat Alone*, tells the story of how he decided to outsource the sending of Christmas cards to a firm specializing in this type of job. He became aware that his database was less than perfect when he received a call from a client thanking him for all three of his Christmas cards, each with a different signature, none of which appeared to be in his own handwriting. For a good step-by-step 'how to' guide to networking, Ferrazzi's book is a fine choice. Another is *Network Your Way to Success* by John Timperley. In both cases, a key to success is 'keep at it' in a planned and focused manner.

2. Positioning yourself as an expert

We all prefer to work with experts; it gives a feeling of confidence and makes it more likely that we will say 'Yes' more rapidly and with less regard to price as a selection criterion or determinant. That does not contradict my earlier statement that technical expertise alone is not why clients hire you and that the strength of the relationship is paramount. If the client is a senior partner in a law firm looking for a consultant to help enhance that firm's business development capability, it is quite likely that he or she would be more willing to engage with or even to seek out a consultant who had written a book on the subject.

Expertise is a matter of perception: it is how the client sees or perceives the expert and the credibility of the factors that imply or confirm their expertise that matter. This is essentially another aspect of being visible to the type of client with whom you most want to work. You must become visible in locations where those clients themselves can be found, which means in online discussion forums and blogs plus as a published author in some form.

In forums and blogs, you may host the forum yourself or make posts on your own blog. Both are great ways, over the medium to long term, to raise your profile in your field. However, do not ignore opportunities to post on forums or blogs hosted by others. In the same way as asking good questions following a seminar session, it can be equally useful to offer succinct, relevant and interesting insights in answer to questions raised on a discussion forum or in answer to a blog post. Obviously, it is essential to abide by the terms of the relevant blog or forum in any post you make. Some may prohibit commercial posts of any kind. However, few if any will preclude you from adding the URL of your own website as part of your signature block.

We have already mentioned YouTube® and the benefits of publishing a series of short video clips there, with links to your own website. You can of course post links to those clips as part of a post in a blog or on a forum. A by-product benefit is to enhance the search engine ranking of your own website if there is an organic link from a third-party website.

As a step up from blog and forum posts, you may consider writing something like a Tips booklet. I have produced two such booklets in the past at the request of clients; one on the topic of leadership development (*Leadership Can Be Learned*) and one on ensuring that your business thrives in an economic downturn (*Doing Well in Tough Times*). Both were used as giveaways to existing and prospective clients and acted as a greatly enhanced business card. A friend of mine, based in California, has made her living out of selling her own Tips booklet and helping others to do the same over many years.

To write a book confers immediate credibility as an expert in the relevant field. It may be either a hard-copy book or an e-book. For those born before about 1980 the hard-copy version is likely to have more substance even if the information in the e-book version is identical, but the advent of the Amazon Kindle™ is beginning to change the way in which the written word is consumed. A book is a great way to evidence your expert knowledge.

Books can now be self-published with relative ease and several services exist to enable anyone to do so who can submit electronic files online in the necessary format. The result can be printed in very low volumes and effectively on demand. If you are fortunate enough that a publisher is willing to accept a proposal from you to produce a book, you can be assured that the result will be professionally printed with the appropriate look and feel. If you adopt the DIY or self-publishing approach, be aware that not all printers offer the same standards of production. Ask to see a sample of 'one they did earlier' and ensure that it meets your standards. The website that supports this book, **www.professionalsbusinessdevelopment.com**, offers a downloadable white paper on self-publishing.

3. The discrete use of PR

PR or Public Relations is not the same as advertising but can help you to become known in much the same way at lower cost. To use PR successfully, it is not necessary to have established contacts in the press, radio, TV, etc. It is essential to understand what the journalists who produce content for these media need and in what timeframe. It is certainly true that journalists, regardless of the medium in which they work, are always interested in a good (ie interesting and attention-grabbing) story that is relevant to their audience. So long as you can identify media that are consumed by your 'perfect' clients and can offer such a story at a time when it is of use to the journalist, there is a fair chance that it will be used.

However, with PR you do not control what is produced. You may give a journalist what you feel is a great story, pre-packaged as a well-written press release. The journalist may take a different view of that story and present it in a very different light than you had intended.

As with becoming a published author, it is entirely possible to follow a DIY approach with PR and to achieve some success. It requires some work and some planning plus an understanding of the mechanics of the journalist's world. You can of course outsource it to an agency. In my experience, it is worth trying the DIY approach first unless your own pockets or those of your firm are very deep.

One useful way to leverage your expertise is to register with the website **www.expertsources.co.uk**. This is used by journalists to locate experts on almost any subject who are willing to be interviewed or to produce information about their field of knowledge or work. You can certainly ask to be acknowledged as the source within an article written on the back of your input. It may not always be credited as such but will be more often than not. You may also want to look at **www.helpareporter.com**, otherwise known as HARO (which stands for Help A Reporter Out). It operates by way of a daily e-mail containing requests from journalists for specific help on particular (often obscure) topics. At one point I wrote a quite lengthy piece in response to a request for help with information about the investment potential of AK47 rifles (short answer: probably very limited as the AK47 was, by a large margin, the most common military rifle in the world at the time). There is more information on the use of PR on the website, **www.professionalsbusinessdevelopment.com**.

4. Online search

The term 'online search' is often felt to be synonymous with 'Google®'; one of the few company names to have become a verb, another being 'Hoover' – at least in the UK. Online search can work for you in one of two ways: organic search and advertising via a PPC (or CPM) approach such as Google®'s Adwords programme.

Organic search is a simple concept that can be hard to leverage. It is also called 'SEO' or Search Engine Optimization. It relies on your website having sufficient content that is relevant to given key words and having external inbound links (ie other sites showing links to yours) that it rises to the top of the results shown by Google® when those key words are searched by an individual.

SEO has become something of a science and is sometimes thought of in terms of how to 'cheat' Google®. The reality is that it is very hard to cheat Google® for any length of time even if it may be possible to achieve a temporary advantage. Google® has for some time focused on good and relevant content as the main way to prioritize the appearance of web pages in its results. It has begun to penalize pages that simply replicate content that has been published previously elsewhere and also those pages that are apparently pure sales pages. The algorithms that drive the search results of Google® and other search engines are updated frequently. If you wish your site to rise to the top of Google®'s results, the best approach is to add good and relevant content regularly.

PPC and other advertising online is again a relatively simple concept but not always easy to do well and in a manner that is cost-effective. For an outline of Google®'s Adwords programme, visit Google® and click the Advertising link, currently located at the bottom of the Home page.

5. The importance of a list – and how to build one

For anyone involved in traditional marketing and selling activities, one of the most valuable tools you can have is a large and growing list of contacts. The theory is that, by electing to contact you, perhaps in response to an advertisement, each person has indicated an interest in a certain type of product or service. If they do not actually buy that product or service after that initial expression of interest you can then contact them more or less regularly (usually by e-mail these days as the cost of delivery is almost zero) until, as a client of mine puts it, they 'buy or say "Goodbye"' and remove themselves from your list.

In the professional services world, it is usually far more effective to target your client acquisition in as focused a manner as possible, in the interest of saving time and effort and increasing the quality of each interaction with each client or prospective client. However, it is still helpful to build a list of contacts who have at least self-selected to the extent that they have made contact with you regarding a specific aspect of your services. So long as the contact, response and follow-up can be automated there is very little overhead in terms of cost or effort on your part.

That can be done simply by adding a data capture form on your website into which a visitor can enter their name and e-mail address, usually in exchange for a report or 'white paper' that provides information relevant to the type of clients you seek to work with. If you are an accountant specializing in helping medium-sized businesses to minimize their tax bill, the white paper could simply highlight a number of errors that such businesses are known to make in the way in which they organize their finances which, if addressed, can reduce their tax liability. That white paper would form part of your own 'marketing collateral' (which we examine in Chapter 4).

Once the initial contact has been made, you will of course need to decide how best to follow up. In most cases that can be done by the use of the auto responder software to send a series of e-mails with additional information that should be relevant to the potential client and encouraging them to make direct contact with your firm. It is a rule of thumb in e-mail marketing circles that this approach will usually require several contacts from you – it can be up to seven – before the recipient will either make a purchase (if you are selling a product) or make contact with you.

This type of approach can be useful in broadening your business base. Some businesses rely on it for the majority of their work. However, for most professional services firms it is best thought of, in my view, as a useful adjunct rather than as a primary source of new clients. Any contact that you gain in this manner needs to be included in your network-building and -nurturing process. It is not a good idea to allow any contact that passes your initial 'potential client' filters or has made contact with you because you have passed their 'potential commercial fit' filter, to fall by the wayside due to lack of effort and interest on your part.

In this chapter we have explored some of the basics of locating and making an initial contact with the right kind of clients for you and your business. In the next chapter we link this to the development and delivery of your own personal brand and that of your firm. The aim is to ensure that there is con-sistency between what the client needs and wants, what you are able to deliver and your cultural fit. The benefit is to minimize friction in developing your relationship so that you can work together more easily and enhance the level of the relationship to that of a true business partnership where there is mutual value.

Your brand: development and management

04

Why is your brand important? It defines in the mind of your clients and prospective clients what it will feel like to work with you. If you are to live up to that brand promise, it will inform if not actually dictate the strategy and the design of your business, its systems and the way in which you deliver value for clients. It must be realistic and authentic for you, because it will set the standards by which you will live and work in your business life (and perhaps also your personal life). Ultimately, your personal brand and your business brand should become interchangeable.

A failure to deliver on your brand promise will destroy your credibility with almost unbelievable speed. With that in mind it is helpful to design and develop your brand effectively at the outset, because changing it creates distractions and dissonance for your clients and may even call into question your credibility in your chosen role.

What is a brand?

The meaning of the term 'brand' has become unduly complex in the minds of marketing professionals for whom it has taken on an almost mystic aura: 'If we can only get the brand right then we're home and dry!' Despite Luddite tendencies among many who are not marketing professionals, much is invested by professional services firms in 'brand development': logo design, creative strap-lines and slogans and of course colour schemes that are carefully chosen to reflect abstract 'core values' such as *solidity* or *youthfulness*. There is then the additional complexity of 'brand positioning' versus 'brand identity'.

Brand *positioning* is, conventionally, the distillation of:

- what you wish to stand for;
- what core idea gives you a competitive advantage; and
- how you want to be described by your clients.

Conventional brand *identity* covers issues such as:

- having a clear organizational structure that clients find easy to understand and that makes it easier for them to deal with you;
- what you represent (to your clients);
- your visual identity and tone of voice (at the organizational level);
- differentiating factors.

The latter two points embody your brand positioning and reflect the strategic thinking of your firm and how it proposes to interact with its clients. Clearly, there is considerable degree of overlap between identity and positioning – at least to someone who does not claim to be a marketing professional other than in a purely amateur sense (and in the true meaning of that word).

In my experience, it is perhaps more helpful to think of your brand (see Figure 4.1) as the convergence of:

- benefits that you are able credibly to deliver;
- problem (or dream) in the mind of the client (plus the perceived solution or fulfilment means);
- values and behaviours.

FIGURE 4.1   The composition of a brand

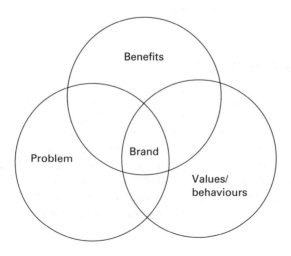

The last bullet point is vital and operates two ways: you to the client and vice versa. Congruence of values and behaviours is as essential for your brand to be relevant to the client as it is for you to be able to work together successfully.

There is one further element that must be considered: the way in which your brand is made real to the client. This is about its practical execution or implementation by way of your business systems and delivery processes. These determine how it will 'feel' for the client and indeed for you and your colleagues when you work together. The key is consistency as well as effectiveness. As an American friend of mine said of the haircut provided by his usual barber: 'It doesn't have to be the best; just the least worst in this town. But it has to be the same each time I go, or else I'd have to worry about how it might turn out.'

To be the 'least worst' is not an aspiration that I recommend; on the contrary to be the best that you can is far more likely to lead to success. However, from the point of view of a client, it is likely to be more attractive to have a consistently 'good' experience in working with you than one which is by turns stellar and abysmal – or stellar versus just OK. Consistency touches a need in many business managers for certainty and 'no surprises'; the idea that working with you is not going to keep them up at night – even occasionally. In my experience, few clients seek to increase levels of risk in their business and inconsistency of delivery is usually perceived to represent additional risk.

The brand is you...

In the professional services industry, the brand in the mind of the client is almost invariably represented by you yourself. It is not really even about your firm as such. In the mind of the client (which is where it matters), there is no such thing as 'a firm': only you – the individual who sits across the table from them and who to them at that moment represents your firm in their eyes.

In order to be positive, the client's perceptions of the 'brand' of that person must, a) be congruent with their own values and, b) be consistent with the perceived brand of the firm that person represents. To be relevant to the client, that brand must also reflect the possibility of a credible solution to a felt need, and the need has to be felt in that moment.

Prior to any initial meeting with you, if your firm is well-known in its field, its generic 'brand' may engage the client, provided that they themselves can identify a problem to which they believe your firm might offer a solution. If the client is in need of a commercial loan, for example, they are likely to welcome a visit from someone with a major bank and who appears to be in a position to grant that loan or to arrange for it to be granted.

In other words, the client will identify an issue and begin to form a concept as to who might resolve it and how, based on their knowledge of the market and the firms they perceive to be leaders in it. In this context, the 'brand' of your firm means the client's perceptions (whether accurate or not) of your firm's values and behaviours and what it will feel like to work with it, as well as the basic commercial opportunity. The firm's name on your business card will therefore gain you access for an initial meeting, but no more. (We look at how to maximize the probability of success in such a meeting in Chapter 7.)

In most cases, your firm's brand is a secondary factor in a client's buying decision. The client will be much more influenced by what they perceive as your personal brand, which is of course an entirely subjective view.

Building your brand statement

In developing your personal brand positioning, it will help to consider:

- What is the role that you would most desire with your 'perfect' client (as defined by the exercises in Chapter 2)?
- What are the likely traits and characteristics of an excellent performer in such a role?
  - How well do you match these? (Be realistic: an above average rating would be 6 on a scale of 1–10 and a 9 indicates performance better than 99 per cent of human-kind.)
  - If you rate yourself lower than 7 on any of these factors, to what extent can you develop yourself to achieve that level? How?
- What results must be achieved to support your desired role? To what extent (on a scale of 1–10 where 10 is high) do you feel confident that each of those results can be achieved routinely? Can you overcome any shortfalls? How?
- What factors define your personal values and behaviours?
  - What are your preferences and 'hot buttons'?
  - What will you *not* do regardless of difficulty? (In other words what actions will you 'never' undertake even if it causes you to lose a client? For example, I refuse to coach executives who have a history of bullying junior staff, not simply because bullying is, for me, a 'hot button' but because I know I am unlikely to coach them well as a result.)

Once you have written down answers to each of those points, you can begin to develop some branding statements that describe what you will 'be' to your clients, not simply what you do. For example, we know that FedEx delivers packages. Its brand statements tell us that it does so worldwide, on time and that we can trust it ('The world on time', 'Relax, it's FedEx').

The final bullet point in the list above is important because it begins to define how you see yourself as a person and the way you decide to go about things. This in turn will help you to design your own personal Unique Selling Proposition (USP).

If you find yourself struggling to articulate some of these ideas, it may help to undertake one of the mainstream psychometric evaluations such as MBTI (the Myers Briggs Type Indicator, or simply 'Myers Briggs') or one of the various versions of the DISC tool. The benefit is to find some 'safe language' that you can use to describe yourself and how you interact with others. MBTI evaluates four pairs of factors:

1 Introversion versus Extraversion (I/E).
2 Intuition versus Sensing (N/S).
3 Thinking versus Feeling (T/F).
4 Judging versus Perceiving (J/P).

Each pair represents a continuum rather than a binary choice and represents preferences that can shift over time and under stress: these are not absolutes. They are an attempt to describe how you 'are' naturally as a person. That description is expressed in terms of a mix of one letter from each of the four pairs of letters: for example 'INTJ' or 'ENFP'.

The I/E dynamic has been described as being battery powered versus solar powered and reflects how an individual processes new information or new experience. An 'I' will seek to reflect on it and will test it against past knowledge and experience. An 'E' will seek to discuss it with others. 'N' people have a desire to envisage broad possibility which may be abstract whilst 'S' people prefer (literally) to get their hands around something. 'T'hinking represents a preference for logic whilst 'F'eeling is about an emotional response. 'J' people take tough decisions quite rapidly whereas 'P's like to see the world as they feel it ought to be.

The DISC tool has some correlation to the MBTI but looks at four different dynamics: dominance, influence, sustaining (or supporting) and compliance. (DISC also has some correlation with the Kiersey Temperament Sorter® – see **www.kiersey.com**.) Both MBTI and the DISC tool use sets of questions where the answers are either binary or by selection from a set of multiple-choice statements. In DISC, the results are presented in the form of a graph with the degree of positive or negative variance from a norm shown by a plot above or below the horizontal norm line; see Figure 4.2 for an example.

Depending on which source you use for your DISC questionnaire, that graph may be supported by a report interpreting the raw data and adding what can be quite significant insights into current stress factors. In terms

FIGURE 4.2 Example of a DISC profile

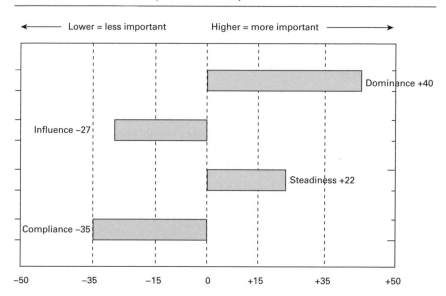

of how to describe each of the DISC components, I have heard it expressed as a set of statements:

D = 'Be brisk, be bright, be gone.'

I = 'Let's get together and team up!'

S = 'Are you OK? How can I help you?'

C = 'This item must be measured to an accuracy of +/– 0.005 mm.'

Both MBTI and DISC questionnaires can be found online. I use the DISC profiling tools at **www.axiomsoftware.com**. The 'lite' versions of both can be taken online free of charge. However, while the results may be of some use in helping you to find safe words to describe your own values and behaviours in this context, they cannot be considered definitive.

Hot buttons to brand promises

In my view, your 'hot buttons' and what you will *not* do no matter how difficult it may be (see the example regarding bullying above) are critical in establishing your personal values and informing your personal branding. The hot buttons may be relatively superficial on the face of it – a lack of punctuality for example can be deeply irritating for some people but of little importance to others. If it is an irritant to you, the question is 'Why?' It may be taken as a lack of respect for your time or a lack of respect for you personally, or both. That may indicate a wider lack of caring for others; perhaps not so unimportant after all. The hot button is about you and is an indicator of the way you wish to interact with others and expect them to treat you. In terms of your branding, that hot button could translate into a brand value along the lines: 'We do things on time'. Indeed, a slight variation on that branding statement is already in use by FedEx: 'The world on time'.

Having answered the questions in the list above and examined your personal 'hot buttons' (and considered the output from one or more psychometrics if you wish), the next step is to develop a small number of branding statements that describe how it will feel to the client when they work with you. These should be no more than a single sentence and can be a short phrase. You may have more than one, but each must be consistent with the others and they must be authentic for you yourself. For example, FedEx uses:

- 'The world on time'
- 'Relax, it's FedEx'
- 'When it absolutely positively has to be there overnight'

These can be used almost interchangeably and although each conveys a slightly different idea, the overall feeling in the mind of a potential client is similar and can be connected logically: global delivery capability, low risk/trustworthy/safe, and punctual.

You should be happy to talk about yourself and your work in the terms outlined by your own brand – but you have to be able to make it real for the client in terms of their experience of working with you. In my own case, for example, I sometimes talk to prospective clients in terms of 'seriousness of purpose but levity of approach'. If I do so, I have to ensure that the client comes away from our meetings feeling uplifted, even if not actually with a smile on their face (delivery of the brand promise).

Your role and the value in resolving pain or delivering dreams

As mentioned above, clients buy because they have some kind of 'pain': a problem they would like to resolve and/or because they have a dream they wish to fulfil. In some cases the problem and the dream are different sides of the same coin. The recognition of a problem may indicate that the client is operating in a mind-set of 'being in trouble' whereas the desire to fulfil a dream usually indicates that the client has an expectation of growth in their business. The solutions that they have in mind will usually reflect these differing mind-sets (eg, cost containment versus possible investment). Any solution that you propose must be framed in those same terms if it is to gain acceptance.

The client will usually have in mind a picture of the kind of solution they seek. It may not be a fully-formed image but there are likely to be some key elements in place; certain outcomes which, if achieved, would represent success. Sometimes, your marketing activity can create (or at least develop) a felt need: for example a poster showing a cold drink with ice in the glass and condensation visible on the side can trigger a feeling of thirst on a hot day.

However the problem or dream manifests itself in the mind of the client, they will take a buying decision and will buy from you only when the following conditions are met:

- They have formed sufficiently positive perceptions of you (and indirectly of your organization); there is a basic 'liking' of you personally (which can be extended to fundamental 'trust' – perhaps over time).
- They believe that you have understood 'where they hurt'.
- They believe that you have an idea of the kind of solution that will work for them (and it correlates with what they themselves have in mind).
- They understand the value (or benefits) that you can deliver.
- They can visualize the (positive) results they will experience if they agree to work with you.

All of the above relate to the role that you seek with the client, which is not in fact the same as 'what you do' (nor is it quite the same as your 'brand', although there is some correlation). You may be trained as a management consultant, but with a given client your role may be in the field of 'Business complexity reduction'. You may be qualified as a lawyer but in the client's eyes you may be a 'Litigation avoidance specialist'. For many of my clients, I have become their 'Virtual chief operations officer'. The key is not what you do. It is your ability to build on basic 'like and trust' and articulate the value you deliver in terms that align with the benefits that the client seeks. Success develops as you begin to link the benefits that you can deliver to the known personal and psychological drivers and needs of the client, using language that resonates with them.

That may sound a little cerebral. We shall explore exactly how you do this in practice in Chapters 5 and 7. However, the benefit of getting this process at least reasonably right is to reduce the natural friction of business development and make it easier for the client to say 'Yes' to your proposal to work together. That in turn starts a process of moving your relationship away from transactional supplier towards partnership, which is the Holy Grail of the professional services world.

Once you begin to work with the client, the infrastructure of your firm comes into play as your process of delivery ensures that what you promised is in fact achieved and hence that what you say and what you deliver are consistent. What you say at the proposal stage resonates with the client because you use language that is appropriate to their mind-set, keys into their learning preference and how they make buying decisions and aligns with their psychological drivers. They are able immediately to visualize the value you will deliver and are delighted that what they experience is consistent with that expectation – even if it is initially only at 'least worst' level.

Value is an important concept. Many people use the word 'value' inter-changeably with the word 'benefit'. In my view, the term 'value' can be better defined as:

$$\frac{\text{desired benefits (as defined by the client)}}{\text{(financial cost + hassle)}}$$

Each client will define value differently. Each of the components of that simple equation changes over time, so value is dynamic and the client's view of it will inevitably be subjective. It is unwise to assume that you know what benefits a given client seeks, which is why the approach to running initial meetings that I recommend (see Chapter 7) involves asking questions at an early stage to identify 'what drives the client' and how they define success. The answers should give a good idea of the benefits that are relevant to them and the specific results they wish to achieve. Your eventual engagement by the client and the success of that engagement derive from those answers.

Linking brand promise and value delivery

Every aspect of your business must be congruent with your brand. The client must experience what you promise by way of your branding statements. If your brand is about delivery on time every time, it is essential that each and every package you collect from a client arrives at its destination in good order, not later than five minutes before its deadline. Each element of your business process must support the achievement of that aim.

In my experience, the simplest way to link your brand promise to the delivery and value that the client will experience is to start by defining the outcome or results that the client seeks and which you have agreed to deliver. If there is more than one desired result, treat each as a separate process (although they may overlap in practice).

Starting with the end result, work backwards to design the way in which it will be achieved. In most cases it is easiest to do this in a visual format, as outlined below. If more than one person (you) is to be involved in the delivery, bring the whole group together in designing the process, if practicable. If you do not actually 'own' any element of the process, it is essential to bring in a representative from the department or external firm that will be doing that part of the job to ensure that expectations are clear to all concerned.

In mapping out or 'backwards planning' a piece of work, I recommend fixing a strip of ordinary brown wrapping paper to a blank wall using either masking tape or BluTack. (Be aware that either, if left in situ too long can increase in adhesion and remove paint or wallpaper when you pull them away.) I then use fairly large Post-it® notes, usually 3 x 5 inches in size, to capture each step in the process. Each can be attached to the strip of brown paper and re-ordered as necessary until you have created a linear representation of what is to be done to achieve the desired result. The more detailed it can be, the better.

Once you have what in business school could be called a 'herringbone' map of the delivery process, you can add a second row of Post-it® notes in a different colour to show the timeframe. That will help to ensure that you achieve the aim on time. Next you could add a row of different coloured Post-it® notes with cost items (we are now on time and on budget). That can be followed with a breakdown of each delivery step into its component parts and specific success factors. Eventually you will create a complete picture of how you can make real your commercial promise to the client ('Here's what we'll do for you and this is the cost') in a manner that reflects your brand promise ('We work on time and on budget and we'll do our best to make it fun for you and for us').

The linking of business systems and processes to your chosen brand goes far beyond the tactical delivery of a particular result for a given client. Your whole business design and infrastructure need to ensure that you can deliver the same kind of experience to every client. Every client that works with you should be able to feel that they have experienced your brand in action. Ideally they should also be willing to say so publicly; but that is another story (see Chapter 9).

Brand and culture: similar but not the same

If your firm is more than a one-person band, it will be essential to ensure that everyone in the business buys in to its brand and that the personal brand of each person is aligned. Not only does this make it easier to work successfully with your chosen clients, it makes it far easier to work successfully together and to enjoy doing so. The larger the business, the harder that alignment can be to achieve at a tactical level. In larger businesses it is more common to hear people talk about 'corporate culture' or 'climate'. These concepts are similar to branding and indeed there is a degree of overlap in what they mean in practice. However, in my view they are softer ideas and do not convey an explicit promise of 'how it will be and feel for you, Mr Client, when we work together'.

In the professional services arena, the culture and climate of a larger firm may be adequate to describe (as opposed to define) the firm's brand at a corporate level, but you yourself will still need to define and deliver your own personal brand, make it relevant to your 'perfect' clients and ensure that you are able to marshal the resources of the whole firm to deliver it in every piece of work you do. The ability to marshal the resources of the whole firm (and indeed of any external partners) to deliver on your promises to clients is the basis of successful strategic account leadership, which, for selected clients only, will underpin the long-term sustainability of your business. (Not all clients can or should be handled as 'strategic' accounts and sheer size is not the best determinant of strategic importance: we explore this in Chapter 9.)

Your USP

All of the above can now come together as you define your USP. The term USP was coined by American advertising copywriter and marketing expert, Rosser Reeves, in his book *Reality in Advertising* (Alfred A Knopf, 1961). He proposed that each successful advertisement, regardless of medium, must offer a specific benefit (not necessarily a tangible one such as cash). That benefit must differentiate your product from the competition and be relevant to potential buyers. It must be sufficient to 'move the mass millions' – ie cause buyers to select your product or service over established competitors.

In my own business, the USP is 'strategy implementation'. It is the explicit linkage of operational delivery to strategic aims and intentions. It can also be expressed as 'operational art', a term borrowed from a Russian military text on strategy dating from 1931 called (perhaps predictably) *Strategeia*.

Many firms focus on strategy, but the vast majority look at the development of strategy. My firm focuses on implementation; on 'getting it done'. By establishing and strengthening the linkage between delivery capability and desired strategic outcomes, the whole firm is enabled to understand not only to what the senior leadership aspires but why and how it can be achieved. Each person can understand their own part in the plan and how their personal success in delivering it can be measured.

How is operational art delivered to my clients? Typically it is by way of leadership development for the client's senior team plus a healthy dose of operational management development. Again, many firms do things such as business process re-engineering. Many more undertake leadership training or coaching. Very few, in my experience, make the explicit linkage between strategic aims and implementation and fewer still add the underpinnings of what I call 'executional' leadership (where the focus is on enabling the firm as a whole to align around a commonly understood and agreed purpose) and operational management, where each activity of the firm is directed to the delivery of a set of benefits for the client.

The combination of strategy implementation and operational art injection appears to be sufficiently unusual as a USP and the benefits are sufficiently clear and tangible that I have made a decent business out of it for over a decade.

Bringing it all together

Your brand positioning, your values and behaviours, how it will feel for clients to work with you, the value you deliver for clients, your brand identity, your desired role with clients and your USP: all are somewhat different facets of the same thing.

They aim to describe or to make concrete the relationship that you seek to achieve with a 'perfect' client. This is important because it allows you to develop a form of words that can summarize these complex ideas clearly and succinctly to potential clients in a way that is likely to be attractive to them. That description, used in your advertising and marketing, will help to generate interest from those who may be potential clients but don't yet know it. Strategic brand development offers the tactical benefit of helping you to answer the first of the three 'killer' questions: 'What do you do?' (The other two questions are 'What makes you different?' and 'Why should I hire you?' and all are variations on a theme of 'Why should I get to know you?'). A helpful approach to structure your answer is to combine, in 75 words or less:

- an outline description of your perfect client;
- their most likely problem or dream;
- your solution.

For example: 'I work with senior partners in law firms who struggle to achieve their strategic aims and grow the bottom line. I enable them to bridge the gap between their operational and technical capabilities and the delivery results that drive success.'

The brand statement (or USP) that you develop is an implied promise that you break at your peril; especially with an established client. It is said that 'Hell hath no fury like a woman scorned'. It is equally true that a disappointed client will not only vote with their feet more rapidly than you can possibly conceive but will also tell up to six other clients or potential clients their story. In a world of rapid and universal information availability, the need to be true to yourself and to your own brand cannot be overstated.

For now, however, we will look at how to have conversations rather than make presentations: conversation is indeed the new PowerPoint®.

Conversation is the new PowerPoint®

05

We have looked at how to evaluate the economic/geo-political context of your clients' business and your own. The benefit is to be able to spot possible commercial opportunities by leveraging your own and your firm's strengths to solve problems and/or fulfil dreams that occupy the mind of your clients. We have explored how to define a 'perfect' client for you and develop a score-sheet assessment tool that allows you to determine to what extent a potential client matches the criteria you have defined. The benefit is to avoid wasting time and effort on opportunities where either you cannot win or, even if you do, the game is not worth the candle.

We have looked at ways to locate good potential clients and ways in which you can be found by them, either online or offline. We have touched on seminars and trade shows, the use of social media and PR and ways in which you can carry out research to identify opportunities where a client that passes your 'perfect client' filter has a clear need ('commercial fit') for your services. We have mentioned ways to approach those clients by highlighting what you perceive to be an opportunity for you to enable them to leverage one of their strengths or to overcome a barrier. We have looked at that opportunity through the lens of your client's customer – the end user of their product or service to consider how you might enhance that offering.

In this chapter we begin to gain traction with client conversations that lead inexorably either to new business opportunities or to your decision not to proceed. If there really is a new business opportunity, these planned conversations will highlight it, and the benefits that you can deliver will be clear. If there is no real opportunity, that too will be clear and it will be apparent to you and to the client that to try to find a way to work together at this time will be 'forcing the fit', which is invariably damaging and leads to poor relationships in the longer term.

I use the term 'forcing the fit' having at one point spent quite a lot of my spare time making furniture. Having cut a joint between a chair leg and the frame and spent time to shape the leg, it is intensely irritating to find that the joint does not quite fit. It may be due to a change in humidity that has caused the wood to swell slightly or simply that you need to shave off a tiny piece of the wood to make the joint fit properly. It is often too tempting to apply pressure – or worse still a sharp blow with the heel of your hand or a rubber mallet – only to see the joint crack. No matter how much glue you apply, that joint will always be weak and liable to fail. It will be a costly error both in time and materials.

Client relationships are much the same: it is invariably better to adjust until a good fit is found or simply bow out until a better opportunity arises. The benefit is to avoid wasting time for both parties. If you explain openly that you are unable to help the client immediately but under different circumstances (which you outline) you could do so, that enhances your credibility and the future potential with that client tremendously. It also differentiates you from most competitors who take the view that 'any revenue is good revenue'. Experience indicates that is not the case.

A benefit of having a conversation as opposed to making a presentation is that you are enabled to explore the commercial fit and ensure that it is a good one (increasing the likelihood of your success with that client). This is because the process of conversation allows you to gather from the client all the information needed to see not only 'where the client hurts' and how you can solve that specific problem but what the client already has in mind by way of a solution (almost invariably the client will have such an idea in mind and if your solution happens to match it, there is a greater likelihood that they will say 'Yes').

You will also learn more about what may be the client's personal drivers at an emotional level and a considerable amount about the way they make decisions, how they prefer to receive information, etc. These data allow you to adjust your vocabulary in describing the benefits you bring so that the words resonate deeply with the client and carry meaning far beyond their dictionary definition.

Perceptions are critical and real (even if they may be incorrect)

Whenever and wherever you meet a client, or talk to them by phone or videoconference, you will always be making an impression on them – creating perceptions – whether you are trying to do so or not. The same is in fact true when you communicate in writing, whether by e-mail or hard copy: however, these perceptions are triggered differently and tend to be more subtle. Broadly we all have different personas we move between as we communicate verbally. These vary from the 'best self' to an alter ego or 'evil twin' (which represent extremes of a continuum rather than a simple binary choice).

Unfortunately, very few people (and especially those who are older and/or senior in their role) truly understand the perceptions they generate when they communicate, especially when they do so verbally. The result for the client can be dissonance, which tends to damage credibility and hence the willingness of the client to do business because it also damages the fundamental personal connection that is based on personal liking and ultimately trust. The latter develops over time but depends on the former. The perception shifts, which can be generated quite unintentionally and unconsciously, need only be quite small and subtle to create sufficient dissonance to lose a sale or make it harder to win an additional piece of work.

If we think of most track sports at professional or Olympic level, the time difference between the gold medallist and silver is likely to be only a fraction of a second. The perception shifts that I have in mind here are similarly tiny. By contrast with the Olympics, in the field of professional services there is very rarely an equivalent of a silver medal: you simply win or you lose. With that in mind, what factors are most likely to lead to the formation of positive perceptions in the mind of the client in that critical first five to 10 seconds of an initial meeting? Why five to 10 seconds? Simply because within that time, perceptions will have been formed which, even if not wholly accurate in fact, will become reality to the individual. Once formed, those perceptions (good or bad) will be hard to alter because we all tend to look for factors that reinforce rather than challenge our initial perceptions, to the extent that they eventually become prejudices.

Authenticity (otherwise known as 'Just being yourself')

The first key factor is to be recognized as authentic or 'being yourself'. There is no complexity here: indeed it should be easy to be yourself at all times. After all, you cannot logically be anyone else, not unless you are a consummate actor and there are very few of them in the world let alone in the field of professional services. To be yourself reduces your felt stress in any new situation; and meeting a client for the first time is of course a new situation. If you feel less stressed, it is likely that your tone of voice will be more relaxed, and we will explore how that manifests to the client later in this chapter. However, any felt stress is audible and even though you may not be listening for it, it will be apparent. If you feel less stress in a meeting, it is likely that the client will mirror this and will also (unconsciously) experience reduced stress.

Many in the professional service field have learnt (or been encouraged to think) that, when meeting a client, they must adopt a 'professional' persona that differs from their normal behaviour. In my experience, the client invariably notices that shift, especially if the client is a woman. For reasons I can only surmise, women appear to have a highly-developed radar for incomplete authenticity and will pick up that slight dissonance almost immediately, with negative results for the 'liking and trusting' quotient. The simple act of allowing yourself to 'be yourself' reduces stress for both sides in a meeting. (Don't forget that the client will experience feelings of stress that are at least as great as your own; it is an initial meeting for them also.) If you can visibly be 'just yourself', the client is likely to relax considerably and the meeting will move forward far more easily.

The second key success factor is that in terms of our communication, whatever feels right for you in any given situation, provided that you are being authentic (ie yourself), is likely to be the best course of action. That in turn raises the third key success factor, which is the recognition that to trust your own gut instincts and rely on your learning from past experience will invariably serve you well. To ignore those gut instincts will lead very often to failure.

For many professionals it may prove hard to acknowledge the reality and value of accessing their own instinct and indeed to rely on it and on experience. Few people who have taken part in dangerous sports or served in any part of the military for any length of time will do otherwise, however. Most will readily accept that, 'If it doesn't feel right, it probably isn't.' Many will forget, though, that if you feel that something is amiss, the client probably feels the same way and it behoves you to try to find out what is going wrong in case it may be possible to resolve it. Sometimes, the simple act of leaning back in your chair and making a light-hearted or self-deprecatory comment will be enough to re-set the situation and remove any unconstructive tension. It also allows the client to talk, which is often a helpful tension reliever and has the added benefit of allowing you to gather additional information.

Tools such as NLP (Neuro-Linguistic Programming) offer ways to understand the mechanics of a client's reaction to any given situation and to respond to it. These approaches offer ideas such as 'mirroring' the vocabulary and body language of the client as a way to engender empathy and a sense of connection, based on the idea that most people favour similarity and look for factors that represent similarity whether of appearance or of views as indicators of connection or identity.

These can backfire. I once observed a much younger colleague who had just returned from an extended course on sales techniques mirroring accurately every change of inflection of the client and each change of position. The client leaned forward, my colleague leaned forward; the client folded his arms, so did my colleague. If the client spoke more loudly and slowly, so did my colleague. It became clear that the client was having fun when he finally adopted a yoga-style lotus position with his ankles crossed beneath him and hands outstretched with thumb touching the tip of the middle finger on each hand. In a falsetto voice and in a mock-German accent, he asked why the young man was not following his lead.

I feel that NLP can be a useful tool, as can many of the other concepts such as analysis of body language that have become popular. However, these things can also militate against being yourself because, unless you are very experienced, you will, necessarily, be thinking about your responses rather than just 'going with the flow'. Given a choice, it is my experience that the act of giving yourself permission simply to be relaxed and authentic and making that visible to a client is of greater value than NLP or indeed any other similar tool.

How will you know when you are 'being yourself'? Many people find it hard to visualize this idea in the context of their work. I therefore use video in early sessions to allow clients to experience at first hand the subtle shifts of speech and behaviour that mark 'best self' versus 'evil twin'. The change may not be 'Dr Jekyll versus Mr Hyde' but even a quite subtle shift is enough to make a noticeable difference to perceptions. Even so, it usually takes some time and practice before they are able to drop into 'best self' mode at will. However, the benefits they experience when they do so (and are able to do so consistently) are so considerable that they usually find it worth the effort needed.

Conversation: a key indicator of being yourself

One way in which it is instantly apparent that you are being yourself is that you speak in a conversational manner. Most people have an idea in their mind as to what represents 'conversation'. It may be that the verbal exchange is not only light-hearted in its atmosphere (the way it 'feels') but the level of discussion is indeed lightweight. They therefore assume that one cannot be 'doing business' by way of a conversation and that doing business equals being ponderous and in 'meeting persona'. Nothing is further from the truth.

The act of having a conversation, as opposed to making a presentation, actually speeds the development of the essential liking and consequent trust that drives successful business relationships. The mechanics of conversation facilitate the exchange of ideas and make it easier for you to find out what drives the client. Conversation enables you to be interested in your potential client rather than seeking to be interesting. It facilitates the asking of questions, in an authentic manner, because questions are one of the key tools of conversation.

Conversation versus presentation

What defines conversation and how does the client experience it by comparison with being on the receiving end of a presentation?

Conversation is essentially two-way while a presentation is essentially one-way, unless it is punctuated by assumptive questions ('Would you not agree that ... ?') which in legal circles would be called 'leading the witness'. A presentation is almost by definition experienced as a monologue rather than as an interaction and hence tends to irritate the recipient unless the content happens to be closely aligned to that person's actual commercial needs and business/psychological drivers.

A presentation is usually based on 'generic product push' rather than 'benefit-based pull'. In other words, a presentation offers a solution to an assumed problem rather than to one that is defined through the process of conversation. In some cases that assumed solution will be sufficiently appropriate that the client will engage with it. The likelihood of that happening is increased by carrying out exercises such as we explored in Chapters 1 and 2 to identify your economic context and what defines a perfect client. These in turn will throw up likely commercial fit opportunities. To the extent that you are dealing with a client where there is a high correlation to your 'perfect' client definition, there is a fair chance that one or more of your generic solutions will work. Most people in professional services will be satisfied with that and feel that it represents a significant enhancement of their business development process. It can be made so much more effective, however, through the process of conversation.

A presentation almost by definition gets in the way of your authenticity. It is hard to go through a PowerPoint® deck, no matter how well you rehearse and how much time you spend with 'presentation skills' trainers and/or out-of-work actors and be perceived as being yourself/authentic. That obviously damages credibility and hence trust and drops you and your relationship down the pyramid to sit among your competitors. You are pigeon-holed in the mind of the client as 'Just Another Boring XYZ' (a 'JAB') rather than as a potential solution provider to a known problem. A conversation differentiates you and rapidly enhances the level of your relationship with the client.

Conversational speech

The key difference between conversation and presentation is, however, in your speech patterns and those of the client. (Indeed it is conversation that allows the client to speak at all; in a presentation they will feel forced by cultural norms into silence while you speak.) During a presentation or when we are in 'meeting persona', we will typically speak in sentences that are fully formed. In conversational speech, we do not. Conversational speech manifests as a series of random word groups and not as sentences.

We learn to read in sentences ('The dog is running.') However, in normal conversation we do not talk in the same way because there is no logical punctuation in speech and no logical start or end to an idea. Our brain will form a concept and attempt to articulate that concept verbally without necessarily having thought it through to the end in a linear manner. The result is a tumbling mass of ideas. These make sense to the listener because they are surrounded by 'para-language' such as facial expressions, tone of voice, visual signals (such as the forming of inverted commas in the air with the fingers). One of the reasons that we typically find it harder to have good conversations by phone is that we lack the visual para-language and can be guided only by the audible cues.

The flow of conversational speech is captured brilliantly by James Joyce in his books *Ulysses* and to a lesser extent in *Portrait of the Artist as a Young Man*. In both cases, what we read here is a written representation of a stream of consciousness which, if read aloud, flows exactly as conversational speech. Within the conventional structure of a novel it is hard to read easily without verbalizing.

These conversational word groups are surrounded by short pauses that go to make up the natural rhythm of speech. Those same pauses allow two things to occur that are critically important for the ability of the client to understand what is being said and to visualize the ideas that are being conveyed.

First, the naturally occurring pauses of conversational delivery allow time for the client to listen and process effectively; there is a small time lag between hearing a series of words spoken and being able to go through the process of cognition. That occurs far more rapidly when we read words. The difference in the speed of cognition is like that between the speed of walking and that of a jet aircraft. The process of hearing depends on a degree of mechanical activity in the ear to convert sound waves into an electrical impulse that is received by the brain. The written word requires no such mechanical activity as the operation of the optic nerve is itself essentially electrical and hence instantaneous for practical purposes. If the pauses that occur in conversational speech are missing, the hearing/cognition process literally cannot keep pace with the delivery of new data and the client loses the thread of what is being said. That problem can be lessened by slowing down the delivery of the presentation, but it will not be eliminated.

Secondly, conversational pauses allow the client to interrupt by asking questions for clarification. Some people will misinterpret these questions as objections. In most cases (unless the tone of voice and wording indicate some kind of aggression) questions are in fact an indication that the client is, a) seeking clarification or amplification and, b) thereby buying in to your ideas. In fact the more the client talks during your conversation the more likely it is that they will feel able to say 'yes' to your ideas, because they have literally 'talked themselves into it'.

Gaze aversion

The asking of questions by the client (or answering one you have asked) will usually be preceded by a phenomenon known in the world of psychology as 'gaze aversion'. The client will look away for an instant and then come out with either a question or a statement amplifying your idea, to which they seek your response. Otherwise they will answer the question you asked.

During that momentary break of eye contact, the client will almost certainly be going through a process of visualizing what they have just heard, thus cementing it in their own mind and allowing them to build their own logical thread of understanding, which is especially important if the ideas under consideration are complex. As the client goes through that process of visualizing, they will almost certainly be unable to hear what you are saying if you simply continue to talk through it, because the brain appears not to multi-task at this level. If you pause long enough for the client to regain eye contact with you, the logical thread will be unbroken and the client will be far better able to follow the linear connection of your ideas and hence to say 'yes'.

Conversation is a two-way interaction that facilitates the asking of questions by both parties, and we explore in more detail in Chapter 7 how you can ask devastatingly effective questions and set up and run meetings that can naturally encourage a conversation. If you ask the right questions in the best possible way, the client will tell you everything you need to know to be able to offer solutions in response to what are now known needs. That approach routinely beats pushing a generic product or service to which you then attempt to retro-fit the issues of the client. Pushing a generic product is akin to trying to force fine wine on an abstainer. It is not sufficient to say, 'I didn't know ...'. As a professional, it is your job to take steps to find out.

Conversational tools

There are numerous approaches to enable conversation to flow smoothly and allow you to gather information about what drives the client at an emotional level (which is where decisions are taken – to be justified subsequently by logic). If you are able to deploy the following consistently, you will experience a major uplift in your level of connection with your clients.

Eye contact

This is vital in order to be seen to engage with the client. It is also essential in order to spot the client's gaze aversion and so pause momentarily and not talk through it. Good eye contact allows you to see when the client is buying in to your ideas (because their body language will change). Typically it will become more relaxed but in some cases the client may become visibly excited. Good eye contact allows you to react appropriately. It also allows you to see signs of discomfort on the part of the client and to pick up signals such as an intake of breath that may indicate that the client is about to speak or is trying to find words to express an idea. If you pause and allow space for them to bring together their words you will undoubtedly learn more than you might have had you simply pressed on regardless. That is of course the key point of any conversation with a client: to learn more about what is going on in their mind.

The nature of your eye contact must of course be appropriate, with normal blinking, looking at notes or papers, etc absolutely required as an element of 'authenticity'. My young former colleague mentioned above also returned from his course with a tendency to lock onto anyone with whom he attempted a conversation with a fixed, unblinking and almost messianic gaze that reminded me of the portrayal of Jesus Christ by Robert Powell in the old film *Jesus of Nazareth*. Needless to say the course provider was not re-hired and my young colleague quite soon recognized that there was a question of degree involved in what he had been told.

Active listening

Listening is one thing, understanding is another. Anne Scoular (author of the *FT Guide to Business Coaching*, and who taught me to coach) described active listening as 'listening to understand, not simply to respond'. To link listening and understanding is the basis for active listening (which is in fact a part of the two-way conversational process). It requires the ability to respond when appropriate; either to ask for clarification or to play back to the client your understanding of what has just been said. The benefit of the latter occurs on several levels. It serves to let the client know that they have been truly heard and understood as well as checking that your understanding is accurate. It also offers an opportunity to build on your understanding in order to offer the client an additional insight that may not previously have been apparent.

Active listening is a skill that is an absolute requirement for those involved in the field of coaching but is also of considerable benefit for many others including lawyers and consultants. Active listening, done effectively, allows you to access the deeper personal and psychological needs of the client far more rapidly and hence to formulate responses or solutions to the issues that are in the mind of the client but may not yet have been properly articulated. This in turn enhances your personal connection with the client and develops the level of trust and credibility.

Authenticity/being yourself

We have already explored this concept in some detail. It is hard to over-emphasize its importance, however. This is, paradoxically, one of the hardest of the conversational tools to use effectively, not least because it tends to go against years of conditioning: the more senior (and older!) the individual, the harder it tends to be for them to give themselves permission simply to be themselves. They may however, feel more comfortable with the idea of 'authenticity' that has become relatively common currency in business/leadership books.

An aspect of authenticity/being yourself that we have not yet focused on is the avoidance of unduly specialized language: acronyms or jargon or 'terms of art'. That is not to say that such terms are to be avoided at all times. Between professionals in the same industry or field, acronyms or terms of art may well serve to shorten and simplify otherwise complex sentences. They can convey specific meaning that is mutually understood. However, to an outsider these same acronyms may be confusing. When deciding what to say, have in mind the audience or the person to whom you are speaking. With a mixed audience, there will be a balance between being seen to talk down to more knowledgeable professionals and confusing the outsider.

Conversational speech

We have examined what conversation sounds like (random word groups) and the fact that its natural pauses allow the listener to keep up with the flow of ideas. Conversational speech simply sounds natural and reinforces the perception of authenticity. It is also by definition more intimate and reinforces a personal connection between you and the client. You will sound more relaxed and that in turn will tend to allow the client to relax and hence become more receptive to your ideas. In conversation, you talk *to* your client not *at* them, which makes it a dialogue of equals, a partnership by implication rather than the teacher/pupil relationship implied by a presentation or lecture.

Silence or pauses

I use the terms 'silence' and 'pause' interchangeably here. The natural occurrence of pauses in conversation allows your client to keep up with your ideas, as outlined above. To allow a longer silence at the end of an idea allows the client to talk. The duration of your conversational silences will seem far longer to you than they do to the client. One of the benefits of video as I use it in early client sessions is to show the positive impact of silence in a conversation. Clearly, to allow silence to extend unduly without a normal conversational prompt or follow-on question is unhelpful: the conversational equivalent of a messianic stare. Sometimes all that is needed is an encouraging grunt or 'OK' to keep the flow of the conversation going.

Silence is without doubt one of the most important of the conversational tools. It is incredibly powerful. If used effectively (but judiciously) it can help your client to express ideas that might otherwise never have seen the light of day. If used to excess, it can kill a relationship almost as rapidly as inappropriate language or behaviour.

Confidence

Confidence is in part an outcome of being yourself and in part an attitude of mind that can be cultivated. There is a difference between confidence in yourself and self-confidence. The latter, taken to excess, can be perceived as arrogance. The former is more to do with quiet self-assurance and determination. Again, either can become a weakness if taken to excess. In moderation, however, confidence tends to support credibility and sincerity, two factors that are critical in ensuring the client's willingness to do business with you, because they are the underpinnings of trust.

Confidence is an outcome of courage (which in my experience is very hard to teach or to inculcate in an individual who lacks it). It can, however, be developed over time but usually only by continually pushing the edges of one's comfort zone and being willing to accept, process and deal with occasional failures and rejection. Not everyone wishes to put themselves through that sort of experience. Indeed, paradoxically, it takes a degree of confidence in oneself to seek to develop greater confidence.

Sincerity

I am told that Groucho Marx said that it is not possible to fake sincerity. 'Not possible' may be too strong a term but it is certainly hard to do so. If one is perceived to be insincere it is usually a terminal and permanent error in the development of any relationship, personal or professional. A potential client will wish to believe, before they commit to doing business with you, that you are sincere in having their best interests at heart.

Sincerity and confidence go together to support credibility, which is not a conversational tool as such but an outcome of the successful deployment of your conversational toolkit. Only when your credibility is clearly established will the potential client be ready to say 'yes'. The client will decide when that moment has arrived. You can do little to hasten its arrival and indeed to try to do so will most likely stop the developing relationship in its tracks. By using your active listening skills, you can usually know when the client is ready to move forward and at what point a period of reflection may be needed.

For a client to say, 'I need to think about this' is not necessarily a rejection signal. It may be that the client quite literally needs time to reflect on the conversation before they are able to take a decision. (In some cases, the psychological makeup of the client – an 'I' (Introvert) in Myers Briggs Type Indicator terms for example – may dictate a need to reflect before taking a decision.) It is also possible that the client lacks the authority to make a decision, which is why it is so important to 'map the client firm', as we examine in Chapter 6.

The new PowerPoint®

I named this chapter with the slightly tongue-in-cheek idea that 'Conversation is the new PowerPoint®'. In an ideal world, PowerPoint® presentations would not be necessary because you have been able to hold good conversations with each of the people in the client firm who are directly involved in or may be able to influence the decision to hire you.

In reality, presentations are a fact of life, not least because some clients feel them to be a necessary means to show that 'These guys have done the work' or because it is a way for them to show colleagues that they have 'been through due process' in making their selection of you and your firm. If each of their potential suppliers has had an opportunity to make a presentation to the same group of people, the process can be seen to have been even-handed. In some cases, a presentation may be a good way to show the client (and of course their colleagues who are their internal clients) progress updates or to present options on key decisions to be taken. We look at the basics of designing effective PowerPoint® decks in Chapter 7.

However, once you have developed the level of your relationship with a client beyond the transactional and even above the level of 'trusted adviser' the need for presentations will largely fall away and be replaced by letters confirming what has been agreed verbally, unless of course you are working in an environment such as government or government agencies where there are legal requirements governing the selection and engagement of external advisers.

It may be that a formal contract is required to confirm your engagement. I recall doing some work many years ago with the Japanese Post Office. The very senior and somewhat elderly gentleman who came to London from Tokyo to finalize the arrangements looked mystified when presented with a draft contract. 'Why do we need this document?' he asked. 'We now have the relationship. That is all that we require.' In reality, although a contract may be a convenient way to document expectations (and indeed expectations do need to be documented), it is a sign that the relationship has become conflicted and hence arguably failed if one needs to refer to the contract again once it has been signed.

And so to understanding complexity and reducing variables by mapping your clients: how to plan your attack.

The wiring diagram of the client firm: seeing the influence connections

06

Decisions are taken by people not by firms; indeed as I have already mentioned, there is no such thing as a firm, only people. While your ability to win business is largely determined by your ability to create an immediate personal connection (liking and being liked tends to lead to trust) with the person across the table from you during the first few seconds of your initial meeting, it will almost certainly be necessary in today's business environment to achieve this more than once to secure business from a given firm. This is because the vast majority of sales in the professional service arena are now what can be called 'complex', in that multiple decision makers are involved.

It is rare in today's business climate that any one person will act as the sole buyer for anything more than a petty cash item such as stationery in a small office. Even then, the decision as to which firm should be the stationery supplier may be one for a group or committee and will be subject to periodic review. In the public sector, almost every item of expenditure is subject to a complex procurement process that is often focused on price and not always on value. It is possible and indeed essential to develop excellent relationships with the individual clients within such a process. Although the relationship may not eliminate competition or the need for a periodic review, it can and will swing a decision if all other things are equal or near equal.

However, it is no longer the case that simply 'getting the CEO on side' will win a piece of work. Several others are likely to be involved at different levels of seniority in the client firm. Each will have a different role in the decision-taking/buying process and you must be able to identify the person in each of those roles and develop a separate relationship with each one in order to maximize the certainty that you will win an initial piece of work that can be leveraged into a long-term, true business partnership, if you decide that is how you wish to build the relationship with that client.

It can be hard to control your point of entry into a potential client firm. If your 'perfect' client is a mid-sized firm of solicitors, you may meet a senior associate from exactly the right type of firm at a seminar. She herself will probably not be in a position to make a buying decision but she will undoubtedly be able to refer you internally to a partner (perhaps the managing partner) who could do so. She is therefore acting, initially, as a gatekeeper; it is her decision whether or not to refer you internally, but not whether to hire you. As you broaden your contacts in the firm it is possible that she may transition into a different role and become your internal ally.

In this chapter we explore the various key roles that you must understand within a client firm so that you can draw a map of your path to success in winning work. If you do not 'map the client' it is likely that you will miss out on some vital information and/or simply fail to understand either some internal politics that could derail you, or misinterpret who is really taking buying decisions and who is simply endorsing a decision made elsewhere.

The primary buyer with the NABAC

In every sale process there will be one person who acts as the primary buyer. In theory that person is the only decision maker whose opinion matters because they have the over-riding vote on whether or not to hire you. In reality, the position is very different and the 'one decision maker' situation is now, in my experience, almost unknown.

The 'primary buyer' is the person who has the 'NABAC' (in other words the specific Need, the Authority, the Budget Availability and the Control to sign off on a piece of work or on a hiring decision). Several others will be involved in the decision to hire you and your firm, however. Each will have a different role in that particular deal. Some may have more than one. Even if an individual is not the primary buyer, they may have sufficient influence to delay or to derail the deal. It is essential to be aware of these sources of influence and to map out:

- Who they are.
- Where they are (geographically and within the corporate structure and hierarchy).
- What their role is in the organizational hierarchy.

- What their role is in relation to a given piece of business that you aim to win (recognizing that this may change over time and from deal to deal).
- What their mind-set is (in other words, how they see things generally).
- What drives them at a deep emotional level.

The benefit is that you can then manage each element of the influence web that surrounds the deal and minimize the probability that it will be knocked off track. We look at the latter two bullet points in Chapter 7. In this chapter, we focus on mapping the first four factors.

For the avoidance of doubt, the days when one simply got a meeting with an individual in the 'C Suite' of a potential client organization, made a knock-out pitch and walked away with a done deal are long gone, if indeed they ever really existed. It would be unwise to think that there is a single sale process or stream of work that delivers a deal. You should expect there to be multiple sales processes going on simultaneously in any given client organization. Each must be planned and managed independently to ensure that they all arrive at your desired end point at near enough the same time.

It will always be dangerous to assume that any of these simultaneous buyers is and will remain on your side unless you manage each relationship sufficiently closely. So, how to begin mapping the various types of relationship and assessing each one? In my own work, I think in terms of the following potential roles within the client firm:

- primary buyer;
- technician;
- end user;
- gatekeeper;
- FOO (from the military acronym for 'Forward Observation Officer');
- antagonist; and
- ally.

Each of these roles can change over time as the level of your relationships within the client firm changes. Each may apply only to one specific piece of business or even to one aspect of it. A particular individual may therefore have more than one role within a given transaction as the deal progresses. This sounds complex and indeed it is not simple. However, merely being aware of the existence of multiple levels of relationship and being on the look-out for the relevant internal politics will put you ahead of the game.

The person who is your initial primary buyer may not necessarily be the most senior person in the organizational hierarchy. They may be the person with the NABAC in relation to a particular deal or piece of work, but they will be the primary buyer only for this transaction.

If you are an executive coach, for example, your obvious initial primary buyer within a client firm may be the head of HR or of Learning and Development. Indeed if there is a coaching budget, it may fall under the control of the head of HR up to a certain level, above which an additional layer of approval is needed; for example the board or the CFO.

If the chief executive is the person to be coached, he or she may be (for this transaction) the end user. Once you have a successful initial engagement under your belt, the primary buyer may become the chief executive with the head of HR as a technician. The motivation of each of them in relation to you and your role with their firm will change as their role in the initial transaction and in future transactions changes over time.

The various buying roles

Let's look in more detail at each of the roles and explore how they interact.

Primary buyer

The primary buyer is the person who has the NABAC for the engagement that you have in mind at present. In other words, that individual has the authority to make a decision to hire you or to authorize another person to hire you. The primary buyer has a budget available that they control. In some cases, the primary buyer may in fact be a committee or a board. However, one person within that group will normally be pre-eminent and their views will tend to sway the remainder.

Your initial engagement may not yet be defined in any detail but will be the 'commercial opportunity' you see when you decide to engage with a given client, either because they represent a good fit with your 'perfect client' profile or because they have approached you as a result of one of your marketing or networking activities and there seems to be a potential fit for you to do business.

The person with whom you have made contact in the first instance may well not be the primary buyer for their organization in relation to your field of work. If not they may be a gatekeeper in the first instance who becomes an end user, a technician or a FOO over time. (Think back to the example above where the law firm senior associate met at a conference acts as a gatekeeper initially but may become an internal ally over time.) In the event that the role of primary buyer is undertaken by a committee (and this is increasingly common in a world where 'good corporate governance' must be seen to be done effectively), it is often a mistake to assume that the individual who will exercise most power in making a decision to hire you is the chair of that committee. That is often not the case. In my experience, the role of the chair can be to oversee the process of decision making and to endorse a decision taken by another individual (often the relevant technician).

That decision is often framed as a 'recommendation' to the committee as a whole. Unless there is dissent, however, it will be accepted and unless the dissent is vigorous, or there is a personality clash, the chair will tend to support the recommendation, which in turn will tend to influence others in favour of it.

Technician

Technicians may well not be primary buyers. However, their influence on decisions to hire you or to do business with you and your firm cannot be underestimated. If you are in the field of IT consulting, the client firm's CTO or IT director will almost certainly be involved in the decision to hire you. Indeed the IT director may take the decision to work with you but must gain budget approval from the board or from the CEO, depending on the amount of money involved.

The mind-set of technicians may not be the same as that of the primary buyer. In many cases their focus will be on risk reduction not just in terms of the operational risk to the firm but more commonly their own reputational risk. The primary buyer may want to hire you due to what they see as your innovative approach. The technician may not see 'innovation' as a benefit but as a risk to be mitigated; hence the old clichés along the lines of 'Leading edge is fine. Bleeding edge is not!'

In this case your approach to – and your relationship with – the two individuals must be managed differently and simultaneously. The hard part is when it comes to making a 'final' presentation to a group such as a board on which both technician and primary buyer sit. Without careful handling, each will expect to hear different things during your presentation. It is much better if possible to avoid the need for such a presentation in the first place by active management of each relationship independently.

End user

If you were in the business of selling office furniture, the end user is, obviously, the person who would sit on the chairs you supply or store documents in the filing cabinets you deliver. In that case, they might be quite junior in the corporate hierarchy. However, they may also wield considerable influence. It is hard to overestimate the impact of a negative comment by the PA of the CEO about a sore back 'from those awful new chairs the facilities director agreed to take on trial'.

It is a mistake to assume that the end user in relation to your work with a client will inevitably be low in the pecking order, however. If you are a lawyer, your primary buyer and your end user may be the same person; the in-house counsel or head of legal. Once again, that person may take a decision to hire you that must be ratified by the board on grounds of the cost involved.

In this example, the in-house counsel may also be the technician, which can add another layer of complexity. Once the engagement gets under way, you may find that a more junior in-house lawyer is nominated as your day-to-day contact for operational purposes. That person then becomes the end user and you have yet another relationship to build and maintain and yet another role to assess and manage.

Gatekeeper

Traditionally, gatekeepers were seen as the PA Dragon who must be vanquished by anyone wishing to see the boss – especially anyone that looked remotely as though they might be selling anything. You may still come across that situation (and there are some simple and fairly obvious ways to defuse it – not least is simply to treat such individuals as though they were in their own right a paying client: a little respect and politeness go a long way). However, in modern corporations, gatekeepers are more often quite senior in their position in the hierarchy and may indeed have primary buyer responsibilities within their specific sphere.

For example, an IT director may have functional responsibility for the selection and implementation of a new CRM application for the firm. It might seem that they are in fact the primary buyer and indeed they may say, 'This is my decision.' It may be their decision in terms of the selection of a solution, but the budget may be controlled by the CEO if a project costs more than a certain figure. If the project budget is above that figure, you now have an additional layer of decision making and relationship building to get through to move forward.

The IT director is in this case a combination of technician (who has decided that your offering is the best technical solution) and gatekeeper – gatekeeper to the extent that they decide how and even whether you are able to approach the CEO. The IT director may prefer to make that approach to the CEO alone, which of course puts your entire project at risk if the relationship between the two of them is less good than it might be or even less good than the IT director thinks it is.

If you know that a glass ceiling exists on budget approvals – an amount above which another level of approval is needed – you may be able to break the project into two parts, each falling in a different financial year, and each therefore not requiring further approval.

It is in any event a major error to underestimate the influence of gatekeepers. They may have no logical involvement in the buying process but may have undue and unseen influence that it will be enormously helpful to harness if possible. A gatekeeper may be anyone that is trusted by someone in any of the other buying roles. They will often be someone who has simply been with the firm for a long time and who 'knows where the bodies are buried' or simply has excellent relationships across the firm. Such a person can help you to cut through vast amounts of internal red tape and politics – if they like and trust you and want to see you succeed because they understand the benefits you can bring to their firm – not necessarily to them personally, although that may help. Such individuals can also become excellent FOOs.

FOO

The FOO (Forward Observation Officer) in military terms is an artillery officer who operates with the troops closest to the enemy. His job is to observe where the enemy are and, when appropriate, to direct the artillery under his control to fire on the enemy. He will then adjust the fall of shot so that it is as effective as possible in neutralizing them. The artillery may fire high explosive, smoke shells or other types of ammunition as the FOO directs. This may either destroy the enemy or provide cover under which your own forces can advance more safely (it is all relative in such circumstances!)

In the corporate world, your FOO will be an individual within the client firm with whom you have developed a good relationship and who is keen to see you succeed in your aims of winning work with their firm. They differ from allies in that they are willing and able to take action and exert positive influence on your behalf, whereas allies are essentially influencers. FOOs will act in your interests only to the extent that they:

- believe you have the best interests of the firm at heart;
- understand the benefits you can deliver; and
- believe that the results you promise can be achieved.

The FOO may be willing either to exert influence directly on your behalf or (more often) to give you information that is valuable to you in framing your approach without breaking normal business confidentiality. For example, it may be helpful to you to know that the CEO plans to retire in 12 months' time and would like to see an acquisition completed successfully by that time as his legacy to the firm. You can begin to frame your approach to the CEO somewhat differently as a result. At one level this kind of information can be basic gossip but at another it goes to form a picture of the client firm around which you can plan your engagement.

The choice of FOO is critical. Be aware that some individuals like to put themselves in the role of FOO because it feeds their ego rather than because it serves and supports you and your aims. If it is possible to develop more than one FOO within a client firm it is helpful to do so. You can then triangulate your view of the situation with theirs and focus on those areas where what you observe differs from what you hear from others.

Antagonist

These people exist in almost every organization. In some cases they simply resist change and any external provider of services is seen as a potential threat to the status quo. In some cases, antagonists are motivated by a genuine concern that your proposed solution is not optimal for their firm and does not address real needs as they see it. In most cases the motivation is less laudable and may centre on issues such as perceived loss of control or NIH ('Not Invented Here') syndrome. Antagonists must be identified as early as possible in the relationship development process so that you can take steps to neutralize their impact so far as possible.

In the Vietnam War era it was often said that you must 'hold your enemy by his belt'. In other words, if you keep your friends close you should keep your enemies closer so as to be able to see what they are doing and how it might impact you and your success. In some cases today's enemies may become tomorrow's business partners; pragmatism taken to the extreme.

Antagonists can become a problem not only before you win a piece of business but mid-way through a project or even after the event. We look at the ongoing management of client relationships in Chapter 9; however, at this point, suffice it to say that an antagonist may not become apparent until your relationship with the firm is well-established. It is dangerous to become complacent and not least because the cause of the antagonism can be misplaced and/or misunderstood.

In one client firm of mine, there was a conflict between the CEO (my primary buyer) and a long-standing senior manager who was approaching the earliest practicable retirement age but still some years away from normal retirement. That person had considerable political capital built up with some senior individuals in the firm's parent company. I had in fact acted to help the CEO find ways to neutralize the conflict issues and hence to keep the manager in a job. After the CEO himself retired, it became clear that the manager had become an antagonist and used his political capital to ensure that a long-standing contract with me was not renewed.

I should have seen that coming and acted accordingly. Antagonists *always* matter, irrespective of their seniority. Failure to be on the lookout for them can cost you dearly, not only in cash terms but emotionally: misplaced and/or unjustified antagonism can be hard to deal with.

Allies

Allies are, essentially, what it says on the tin. They are not simply the reverse of antagonists and it is unlikely that these individuals will be involved directly in an initial buying decision. However, they can become valuable as you extend your surface area with the firm. They differ from FOOs in that they will exert positive influence rather than take direct action on your behalf.

They may be either positive allies or reactive allies. The former will seek opportunities to promote you and the benefits you deliver. Reactive allies will normally voice support only if asked to do so. In most cases allies will emerge only after an engagement process has begun or even after an initial phase is complete and the benefits become apparent. They can be very helpful in maintaining a positive ongoing relationship with the client firm and may in due course become primary buyers in their own right. I have in mind an individual with whom I first worked in 2003 as a young, newly-promoted vice president in a large European insurance company. He is now a regional head in that same firm and I fully expect to be hired by him to help some of his team members in much the same way as I helped him in the past.

Mapping the client firm: a process

When you first make contact with the client firm, your approach may not be to the primary buyer. In most cases, it is not. Your initial step will therefore be to gather information that will help to confirm that there is indeed a good probability of a commercial fit, to begin to identify what drives the client at various levels and to identify the various roles involved. You can then begin to plan an approach to each of the key players.

In my experience, you cannot be successful in winning business unless you have identified and made positive contact with individuals in at least two key roles: primary buyer and technician. In both cases, life will become far easier if you have identified the relevant gatekeepers and begun to develop a separate, parallel relationship with them. It will be considerably harder to be successful if you do not also have a FOO or at least a potential FOO. The more complex or costly the project, the more important is the addition of at least one FOO (it can save considerable time and trouble). If you are able to identify and get buy-in from one or more end users that is helpful. I recommend the creation of a score-sheet to ensure that you (almost literally) have your 'ducks in a row' before you try to move forward, let alone close a sale; see Table 6.1 for an example. Each of your scores is of course subjective. It does no good to over-rate or to under-rate them; being realistic will make your life easier in the long-run.

To enter a score for any role, you must be able to name the individual and have met that person at least once. Your score should reflect what you perceive to be the level of L+T you have at that moment with the individual and how credible you believe they perceive you to be in your chosen role with them. For the technician, it should also encompass how well you believe that your proposed solution meets the needs of the client firm in absolute terms and also relative to the competition; in other words, the extent to which a reasonable person would be content with your proposed solution and see value for money.

TABLE 6.1   Client mapping score-sheet

Role	Name (each role must be identified by name)	Maximum score	Your rating (How positive is the relationship?)
Primary buyer		35	
Technician		20	
FOO no 1		20	
End user no 1		15	
Gatekeeper identified for primary buyer		10	
Subtotal 1		100	
Antagonists (negative scoring for *each one* identified reflecting degree of perceived influence and degree of antagonism)		(20) for each one	
Subtotal 2			
Net Score **Subtotal 3** (Subtotal 1 − Subtotal 2)			
Additions			
End user no 2 (or proactive ally)		5	
FOO no 2		10	
Gatekeeper for technician		5	
Additional allies (maximum two)		10 in total: 5 each	
Subtotal 4		30	
Net Total (Subtotal 3 + Subtotal 4)			

Once you have covered the primary roles, you should consider carefully actual or potential antagonists. Check with your FOO. It may be that an antagonist has not become apparent as yet but that some element of your solution would give rise to friction for a person in a position of influence. For example, it may make perfect sense for the client firm to outsource part of its IT infrastructure. An IT director (who might logically be your technician) may in fact be an antagonist because he or she will lose some of his or her team and a measure of power as a result of the work you seek to do. That person may smile sweetly and say 'Yes of course' but in reality place hurdles in your way.

If you have two antagonists each of whom is highly influential, it will be hard to succeed with a given client firm unless/until at least one is neutralized (you would have a negative score of 40 points to set against whatever your positive score may be). If the total score for 'Your rating' is less than 60, it is likely that you have missed some important information, failed to neutralize an antagonist or failed (at least for the time being) to develop a sufficiently high level of relationship with a key person.

At the least you should treat this as an alarm signal and review what you have learnt in your initial conversations with your contacts at the client firm. If your total net score is only just above 60, even with some of the additions taken into account, it may still be that you need to do further work in one or more areas. If your net score (subtotal 3) is at or above 60 without additions, you should be in a reasonably good position to move forward.

If you have an antagonist who you have not managed to bring to a neutral position and who you fear may be working against you, you should develop a plan to deal with the problem. That may simply be to work hard at building a good working relationship with the individual. If you sense a 'visceral dislike' between you and the person in question (something that occurs rarely and unpredictably) it will be impossible for practical purposes to get over that problem yourself; you should consider that you are the problem. You will have a good idea if this is an issue because such a visceral dislike is usually two-way: if you feel it, so will the other person. If that occurs, the best approach if practicable is to ensure that a colleague becomes involved in that relationship. If possible, it can help if that colleague is senior to you.

Multiple roles

Don't forget that an individual may have more than one role. One of your FOOs may also be a gatekeeper for example. It is also vital to remember that seniority in the firm does not guarantee real influence or decision-making power and, conversely, people in fairly junior roles have surprising influence. You need to do the work to check that what you are told is indeed real.

One of my clients was global managing partner (GMP) in one of the Big Four accountancy firms. My introduction to that firm came via the head of HR who eventually acted as both a gatekeeper and FOO, having initially acted as the primary technician.

One of the gatekeepers to the GMP was (as is often the case) his executive assistant (EA). During my initial engagement with the GMP, it became clear that his EA had some issues on which I was able to offer some help. She immediately became a surprisingly influential and insightful FOO, whose reach across the firm was quite staggering. That FOO role was in addition to her gatekeeper role. I can recall at least one occasion where she actively prevented an antagonist from reaching the GMP until long after it might have been possible for her to do damage to the project on which the GMP and I were working.

Questions to clarify roles

Mapping the client firm after your initial meeting is important in planning your next steps. It is quite likely that the roles you identify at the outset will change over time, with the possible exception of the primary buyer and/or technician; these should be apparent from the start. However, there are times when you can be knocked off track because an individual has misrepresented or perhaps misunderstood their span of decision and hence their role in relation to your engagement.

Many sales professionals will ask a question along the lines: 'So this is your decision?' to confirm that they are dealing with a primary buyer. The individual may say, 'Yes' and be happy to sign a letter of intent or even a contract, only to say, 'That's fine. I've signed it. It can now go off to Procurement for processing.' What they really meant was that they have the ability to say 'Yes' in principle to a solution but the procurement team will then haggle over price and/or delivery terms and indeed process of delivery. In other words the person you thought was the primary buyer is in fact no more than the technician: they lack the critical NABAC. Questions to ask to ensure that the roles of individuals within the client firm are clear include the following.

For primary buyers
- 'You told me that going ahead is your decision. Do we need to take this anywhere else for final approval or budget allocation once you are content with everything?'
- 'Who else needs to cast an eye over this or give it the nod?'
- 'Does anyone else need to be involved?'

For technicians
- 'Are you happy with the mechanics of this solution and the process?'
- 'Are you comfortable that this will fit with your current systems?'

- 'Are you comfortable to recommend this to the board from a technical viewpoint? Does anyone else need to be informed?'
- 'Who else needs to support this from a technical standpoint? Should we go to see them together?'

Change

Change, like the poor, is always with us. Even when you think that you have the relevant roles in a client firm pegged down and the development of the relationship seems to be progressing well, it is a mistake to relax or to become complacent. Change is the only constant in business and relationships that have moved a couple of steps up the relationship pyramid can drop back in an instant. You will always have competition and not always from external sources. It is often forgotten that a client has two options that will not be on your own list: do nothing and DIY.

It may be that neither is as 'good' a solution as the one you have proposed. 'Do nothing' may become an option due to changed circumstances such as a possible acquisition or merger. DIY is often put forward as an option on grounds of cost, especially with IT systems development and implementation. Experience indicates that, in the IT field at least, DIY is rarely the optimal solution unless the system under consideration is small. Nonetheless, in times when cost is an increasingly important consideration it will be an error not to include these two internal options in your planning and to help the client to understand why they may not be effective or necessarily cheaper.

What drives the client?

You now have a mechanism to consider the various roles that will be fulfilled by individuals in any client firm. You will need to treat each as a separate and independent piece of relationship development and orchestrate them to bring them to the point at which a positive decision to hire you can be taken. Ideally each person should feel that they have already taken the decision by that stage and that the final agreement is a pure formality. If that is not the case, although you may well still win the deal, you will probably have missed something that will need to be dealt with as you do the piece of work if you are to move the relationship another step or two up the pyramid. The problem may otherwise come back to haunt you later.

The likelihood of such a problem is reduced if you are able to ascertain not only what role a particular person plays in the decision-making process but also what drives them at a deep emotional level. That can take time unless you change the way in which you run your meetings and also know what information you are looking for, over and above the usual 'commercial needs'. We look at this in Chapter 7.

Maximizing success in your meetings

07

In this chapter we examine how to avoid the common errors that cause most meetings to fail. We also look at how to plan and run meetings so that the success ratio is far higher and the results far more impactful and longer-lasting. The way that you run a meeting tends to influence if not actually to dictate the perceptions of your role. This is especially true in the case of initial meetings with potential clients. Up to this point, we have examined in some detail planning and preparation. The approaches outlined in this chapter represent the culmination of that preparation, where we gain traction and begin the process of changing the way you engage with clients, internal and external, to maximize success in achieving the results you seek.

This approach will work with any meeting and regardless of the medium used (face-to-face, phone call, video conference, etc). It is especially powerful in the case of initial meetings with potential clients. Indeed it can save a huge amount of wasted time and effort simply because it changes the process and ensures that both parties are aligned from the start. If that is not the case, it becomes clear at once and you can adjust the meeting as required – including deciding to walk away. However, if you have followed the process discussed in previous chapters for qualifying and mapping clients, that should be a very rare occurrence.

We will focus on an initial meeting with an external client but the same framework is equally effective for subsequent client meetings and also for internal meetings. In fact, if you begin to think in terms of *every* meeting being a 'client' meeting, it will reduce internal corporate friction tremendously. To treat everyone with whom you interact at work, internal or external and regardless of seniority, as if they were a paying client, changes typical corporate dynamics positively and will make your life easier. It is harder for colleagues to be less than collegiate if they are being treated like clients and any negative behaviour on their part becomes consequently highly visible.

In this chapter we examine how to avoid the typical 'meeting information dump', how to ascertain rapidly and with a high degree of accuracy what drives the client at a deep emotional level, what factors to look for, and how to use this information to present your ideas most effectively. We consider why meetings need to be planned to be successful and how to do that in a way that is simple to do but very powerful. The benefit is to enhance the probability of achieving the results you seek from any meeting. This approach also tends to change your role in the eyes of clients and move the relationship up the pyramid from transactional towards partnership – assuming that is an outcome that you seek (and there are multiple benefits).

Meetings in general

Most people working in the professional services field (indeed many people in corporate life) spend the vast majority of their working lives in meetings, other than when working alone – dealing with e-mails for example. For many of us, the common factor of most meetings is that they feel like a waste of time and are dreaded accordingly. This occurs because most meetings are badly run and/or are held for the wrong reasons. In this section we look at some of those issues.

Meetings may take place face-to-face, in person or by video-conference, or by telephone. Each of the latter two approaches has its specific added issues but each is essentially just a meeting with some intervening technology. It is mainly the intervening technology that creates the added issues. Otherwise, these are just ordinary meetings. A conference call by phone or a video-conference that involves more than one person in each location adds a layer of complexity. The complexity increases in direct proportion to the number of people involved and any time delays that may be imposed in the discussion by the limitations of current technology.

The location of your meeting may introduce additional factors. For example, a 'formal' meeting in a board room feels different from a conversation over a cup of coffee in your favourite café. Nonetheless they are just variations on a theme. All meetings are, in reality, similar to the extent that they involve people talking about a set of ideas and striving to achieve some form of out-come or decision. However, therein lies the first issue: to take a decision is a perfectly logical and valid reason to hold a meeting. In reality many meetings occur for other (much less sound) reasons:

- to 'talk through' information;
- to 'gain consensus';
- to 'socialize a concept';
- to provide the illusion of progress;
- to delegate tasks (but without always delegating the necessary authority or ensuring accountability);

- (occasionally) as a forum in which senior individuals can demonstrate expertise or brilliance.

In many meetings, a significant percentage of the participants do not need to be present and/or could give their input by other means, for example in writing prior to the meeting with questions clarified by way of a pre-meeting phone call.

Meetings are, inherently, not a good forum in which to disseminate information. A possible exception may be an occasion on which the CEO or equivalent briefs the entire workforce on an issue of major importance such as the fact that the firm is about to make a significant acquisition (or indeed is about to be acquired). Such a meeting will normally only be a short explanation of what is happening and (sometimes) why, with any meaningful questions handled elsewhere; it is more a short presentation than a meeting as such. This type of meeting has its own specific issues and although usually short in duration can give rise to untold problems if it is not properly prepared.

A friend of mine who was involved in the acquisition of a fairly significant competitor firm was asked to give a short 'we come in peace' speech to the staff at the acquired firm. Feedback afterwards indicated that the perception generated was far from that intended. He had apparently – and quite unintentionally – given the impression that the lives of all present had been devoid of meaning until that moment and that only now could they arise as if from a magical sleep to fulfil their destiny. As he said, to speak on the back of an eight-hour flight with no formal preparation was, in hindsight, a mistake.

Why are meetings ineffective as a means of passing information? Simply because the vast majority of people can read several times faster than the person addressing the meeting can talk. They can also read at their own pace; break to reflect when necessary and hence digest the information (or at least the key points) more easily and far more rapidly. To provide information in writing is therefore more effective than to 'talk it through'. The purpose of the subsequent meeting (if one is necessary) then becomes to answer questions on the information that has already been provided and to agree next steps.

In most meetings, the information is dumped unceremoniously on the audience/client. Too much information delivered all at once overwhelms the ability of the client to understand what has been said and they will be unable to make a decision – certainly not one that can be considered informed. The reality is that most people do not listen well nor do they listen actively; further reasons why a meeting used to 'talk through' information rather than sending it in advance will tend to bog down. Meetings held to 'gain consensus' or 'socialize an idea' are likely to be ineffective for similar reasons. They also allow an opportunity for far too many people to hide in one way or another and not to participate. They may say that the meeting was dominated by a few strong personalities and they felt unable to be heard. That is in fact a perfectly valid criticism of many meetings where the aim is to take a decision, the number of people present is greater than, say, five or six and the person acting as chair fails to ensure that each person is able to speak.

The excellent book *Time to Think* by Nancy Kline (published by Cassell, 1999) offers an approach that seeks to make it possible – indeed essential – for each person present at a meeting to hear and to be heard. Failure to achieve this will almost certainly lead to a lack of accountability for actions 'agreed' at the meeting but also in many cases to the loss of valuable contributions from individuals who may well be subject-matter experts on a key issue that must be addressed if the project in hand is to succeed. Those contributions may be lost and a project jeopardized if they are not heard.

Delegation of tasks without delegation of authority is endemic in many large corporations, in my experience, and inevitably leads to disappointment, frustration and failure. It can also lead to alienation on the part of the person to whom the responsibility, but not the control, was delegated and who felt unable to push back on what they knew was almost certainly going to become a 'hospital pass' (a rugby term for passing the ball to a team-mate, closely marked by opposition players who will immediately tackle him with the likely result that he is hospitalized). Responsibility without control is invariably a recipe for disaster. Too often a (usually large) meeting will become the forum within which a task is delegated without the relevant control. In some cases the person to whom the task is delegated may be unaware that this is planned prior to the meeting: it comes as a shock and the meeting is too hard a place in which to refuse the task or even to ask questions.

The 'executive brilliance exhibition' meeting seems still to be prevalent in some larger firms. To my mind it represents a basic failure of self-leadership and of self-awareness. I have seen very few instances where an individual is able to hold the interest and involvement of a group of colleagues or clients for an extended period. In those instances, a common factor is that the style of delivery was untypical in that it was conversational rather than didactic. We shall explore that concept in more detail shortly.

In the case of meetings with external clients or potential clients, it is all too easy to become a slave to the PowerPoint® deck that was intended as a support to give structure to a presentation. You go into 'presentation mode', deliver the maximum amount of information as rapidly as possible and simply overwhelm the client's capacity to comprehend and thus take a decision (even if they retain the will to live).

Avoiding problems with meetings

You can avoid these problems by:

1   inverting the usual process;
2   recognizing how decisions are taken and why;

3 planning and preparation;

4 conversation versus presentation (see Chapter 5).

1. Inverting the process

Most meetings (and I include here 'presentations') are run as an 'info-dump'. The apparent purpose is to download as much information and data as possible in the time allotted ('Let's allow for a 10-minute meeting over-run here: there is just so much you need to know.') The information is dropped in a linear, incremental format that requires the listener to follow a step-by-step argument, to understand each step in turn and the connections to the previous and next step, and hence to arrive at a logical conclusion. This tends to be unsuccessful for many reasons and ignores the fact that the desired conclusion will often require an emotionally based decision rather than a logical one, because most decisions are taken at an emotional level and justified by logic post-event.

Research indicates that less than 50 per cent of the delivered information will be retained by those present at the meeting by the end of the following day and that the half-life of the remaining retained information is measured in days rather than weeks unless it is put to almost immediate and repeated use. (Research carried out by H F Spitzer as early as 1939 indicates that only 21 per cent of information is retained after 21 days and that the degradation is almost half – 46 per cent – in only one day.) This typical meeting process runs counter to all the normal rules of thumb of effective communication:

- Most people prefer to talk rather than to listen (or at least to interact rather than be only in 'receive' mode).
- Too much information delivered too rapidly and with no time to reflect and process will usually cause confusion so that no decision can be taken.
- The attention span of most human beings is quite short; probably less than 15 minutes. In my experience the more senior the individual, the shorter the attention span in meetings: probably nearer 5 minutes than 15. In any event the relevant decision will usually have been taken within 15 minutes, regardless of how long the meeting may last.
- It also militates against the achievement of a key aim of oral communication: to elicit a response rather than to pass information.

By inverting the normal meeting process, we place the desired result (the conclusion) at the start of the meeting, ideally in the form of a stated aim plus any specific results that you seek or that you wish the client to take away from the meeting. In the vast majority of cases, the client will simply nod in agreement. They have therefore entered a psychological contract with you to achieve that aim and those results. All that remains is to agree how to do so.

At this point the meeting begins to take on a life of its own. The temptation for most professionals is to leap immediately into presentation mode; to bring out the pitch book or open up the PowerPoint® deck on the laptop. There is a huge feeling of comfort in having a prepared structure in the form of a presentation of some kind. You can learn it by heart. You can practise its delivery until it feels and looks smooth. Sadly, it then becomes as flaccid as a worn-out tie.

There are several problems in relying on a prepared speech. First, it militates against your simply 'being yourself'. By definition, if you are delivering a pre-prepared speech, you are not being yourself. Unless you are a consummate actor, that will be immediately apparent and it will damage the perceptions you create in the mind of the client that engender the basic trust needed to move forward and do business together. In addition, the prepared speech puts you into 'product push' mode where you are seen to be self-serving rather than building a situation in which you and the client co-create a solution to a known set of issues.

The latter approach places you in a different role – one that inclines towards a business partnership as opposed to a purely transactional arrangement – see the relationship pyramid in Figure 7.1. In a transactional situation, success will occur largely by chance because your offering happens to hit a warm if not a hot button: success occurs randomly due to a congruence of time and

FIGURE 7.1   Relationship pyramid

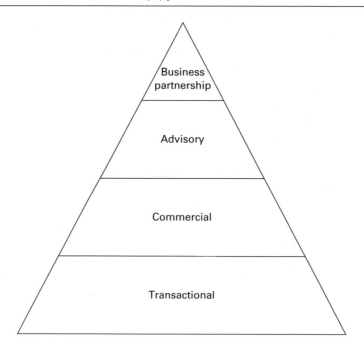

place. In a business partnership situation, price is minimized as an issue and you become recognized as a critical avenue to the success of the client because you bring capabilities that are complementary to those of the client and enable them to leverage a core strength or overcome a strategic or tactical weakness.

The relationship pyramid

Let us take a moment to look at the relationship pyramid. It is helpful to understand this concept at this point because the approach to meetings outlined here enables you to short-circuit the time taken to move up it. There are several benefits of building a relationship that sits at higher levels on the pyramid.

The different levels of relationship are characterized and can be identified by the type of conversations you have with the client and the type of language they use:

- A *transactional relationship* is characterized largely by issues of price and speed of delivery. The context is 'immediacy'. The topic will be a decision taken now with results seen tomorrow or sooner. The product involved will typically be a commodity of some kind, at least in the eyes of the client. That may include a service such as consultancy ('There's a dozen of you guys that can do this kind of work so you need to sharpen your pencil.')

- A *commercial relationship* still features price but also covers issues of expertise, experience, quality and value in the sense of 'cost of ownership'. There is a recognition that, if the relationship is to last for longer than this particular deal, you and the client need to get along at a personal level even if you may not become 'best friends' any time soon. The client is willing to focus on how you can help (differentiated benefits) not simply on the cost versus value-add equation. It is akin to asking for quotes from three builders and not taking the cheapest because you don't instinctively like and trust the individual.

- An *advisory relationship* is based on professional respect in addition to the basic personal liking/trusting necessary to do anything more than a transactional deal. There are grades of status here: 'probationary', 'advisory' and 'trusted adviser'. A probationary relationship will often mean that your advice will be tested (overtly or covertly) against that of at least one other adviser. Indeed being that other adviser may be the role in which you first graduate to advisory status with a given client.

In an advisory relationship your role becomes closer to the client and to the rest of the client's immediate team than in any commercial relationship. You may begin to become involved in decision taking. Pricing of your services is relatively elastic. You will need to be acutely aware of market rates for the kind of work you do. However, so long as there is a clear differentiation between the run of the mill operator in your field and the service you provide, you can set fees towards the top end of that range.

To enhance the advisory relationship to the next level, you may want to consider options such as a secondment to the client's firm. Many larger law firms will embed a bright, newly-qualified lawyer into the in-house legal team of a major client for, say, three or six months. The consequent strengthening of the relationship can be immense. One lawyer I know, who was at the time a partner in his firm, seconded himself, unpaid, to the legal team of a major client during the recent financial crisis when his usual workflow dropped sharply. When times improved he was in great demand from that client firm.

However, in an advisory relationship, there will be an implicit if not an explicit expectation that you will always be willing to take a call seeking advice or to do some background work without necessarily being paid directly for it. In this context, if practicable, you should consider establishing a retainer fee arrangement with the client. The benefit is that, for small, ad-hoc pieces of work, 'the meter does not run' when you are asked for help.

In a *business partnership* relationship, the client recognizes that you are a critical factor in their ability to be successful. They may well tell you exactly that. They will seek and expect help from you as if you were a member of their in-house team and indeed in their minds at that point you are, in all but contractual terms. At this point, the price for your services is highly elastic and you will enjoy almost unfettered access to the client plus strong referrals within their firm and to other non-competing firms. This type of relationship largely eliminates internal politics and also competition in your sphere. It sounds idyllic and indeed it is – so long as it lasts.

Don't expect such relationships to last forever. They are intensely personal and once the person with whom you have that special relationship is promoted or leaves to join another firm, or moves to another part of the country, or retires, you may find that you fall victim to internal jealousies and to the perception that you were 'Fred's key person' and therefore not to be entirely trusted. It is akin to the clearing out of political appointees on Capitol Hill in the aftermath of any change of administration in the United States. For this reason (and many others) it is always wise to extend your personal surface area within any client firm as far as you can without upsetting any existing relationship. Clearly the greater the number of strong relationships you have the better, within reason. However, one can only handle a relatively small number of such intense business partnership relationships at any given time, which is why the concept of strategic account management (or as I prefer to think of it, leadership) is so important; see Chapter 9. Such strong relationships rest always on a knife-edge. They are hard to develop and can be broken in an instant by a failure to appreciate the subtleties of internal corporate politics. I recall one situation where a younger colleague developed an attachment to the PA of a senior client. The lady welcomed the relationship but her boss did not. It quickly became clear that my colleague could not continue to work for that particular client. As the personal attachment flourished so the value of our work with the firm fell away.

2. Recognizing how decisions are taken and why

We take decisions based on emotional factors. The decision may well be documented and if necessary explained in terms of logical process. However, the actual decision almost always comes from gut instinct and is usually binary: buy/do not buy; yes/no.

The genesis of the decision will normally be the recognition of a problem or the articulation of some form of dream or desire. In recognizing the problem or desire, there will usually be an outline in the mind of the client of the kind of solution that would 'work'. When you meet a client for the first time, if there is no immediate 'problem' or desire, there is no immediate commercial fit. That does not mean than there will never be a fit; just that the time is not right now. If, when you meet the client, you can both identify the problem/desire and you offer a solution that aligns broadly with the one already in the client's mind, there is a high probability that the client will want to agree to your proposal. There are three provisos:

a an emotional connection with you personally;

b availability of budget; and

c the client's level of authority to allocate that budget; in other words who else has to say 'Yes'.

To get to the point where it makes sense to offer a solution we need to know four things, ideally:

i The commercial fit and the client's 'in mind' solution.

ii The client's emotional drivers.

iii How the client takes buying decisions.

iv The client's learning preference (how they prefer to receive information).

The first two are essential, the latter two highly desirable. If you know all four and are able to act on that knowledge the probability of success in winning business is very high. It can be helpful to form a view of the client's psychometric profile if you yourself are knowledgeable enough to apply the information. For practical purposes, the four factors listed above will give an effective 80 per cent solution.

The likely commercial fit should be apparent based on the work done prior to any meeting with the client (we began to look at this in Chapters 1 and 2). If the client has a high correlation to your 'perfect client' specification, you will already have a fair idea of where the issues that 'keep the client up at night' will lie. You should also be able to project what kind of solution might appeal. One purpose in your initial meeting will be to test those assumptions and drill down on the reality of the client's situation.

In terms of the emotional drivers, these can be classified as either 'personal' or 'psychological' drivers. There is no hard line between the two. It is probably easiest to say only that the latter tend to be deeper and although perhaps less explicit they are more powerful. An example of a personal driver would be the CEO who decides to relocate the corporate headquarters of his firm to the city in which he grew up; a strong personal driver to 'go home'. Examples of psychological drivers would include:

- a need for power;
- a need for control;
- a need for acceptance;
- a need for recognition;
- high levels of risk aversion;
- the reverse of risk aversion, which has been called 'adrenaline junkie syndrome' or 'fool's courage'.

You will get clues about these factors as well as about the reality of the commercial fit by listening carefully and actively to the questions you ask after the client has said 'Yes' to your stated aim and the results you outline at the start of the meeting. Note that these factors are likely to change over time. The psychological drivers will tend to remain in place but altered circumstances will change the emphasis and degree to which they are present. The type of language that the client uses as well as the ideas expressed will give you clues: there may be nothing that is clear and concrete but this is where intuition or 'gut feel' comes into play. Give it free rein; use your instincts and rely on past experience to guide you, but not necessarily to decide.

Note that, as part of these psychological drivers, there is always the chance that you will find yourself dealing with a client who has psychopathic tendencies. The book *Snakes in Suits* by Paul Babiak and Robert Hare (published by Harper Collins, 2006) reports quite high levels of psychopathic behaviour in board rooms and 'C' Suites in the western world. There seems to be little reason to imagine that this is not replicated worldwide. That same book also provides some insight into factors that might indicate this tendency. If you come across this type of behaviour, it is, in my experience, best to walk away as soon as practicable, otherwise you risk becoming mired in a relationship that becomes emotionally draining and potentially damaging.

Buying decisions are taken in different ways by each person. The 'buying decision matrix' has some similarities with the relationship pyramid. To a degree these decisions are influenced by circumstances; a client facing an immediate and significant problem and who is budget constrained will tend to make decisions in a transactional manner, ie based on price and speed of delivery and will do so independently of your relationship, which may be at a higher level under normal circumstances.

There are four broad buyer types and they reveal themselves by the type of language they use and their focus in your conversations:

a *Transactional buyers* will focus on price and speed of delivery. They will be largely immune to arguments such as 'total cost of ownership', which might indicate a different choice. (Perhaps they were not fortunate enough to have a Yorkshireman for a grandfather, as I did, one of whose maxims was 'Buy cheap, buy twice'.)

b *Informational buyers* will focus on process and ask for it to be explained in linear fashion. They will ask questions about 'how it works', 'how my people will be affected', etc. These people may frustrate those who are less detail-oriented, especially if that preference is combined with strong risk aversion as is often the case (it can lead to 'Not Invented Here Syndrome'). However, if you are able to produce volumes of information and data, that will usually enable them to feel comfortable, not least because they can feel reassured that you 'have done the work' and that they can, if challenged, 'prove' the same to their boss because of the volume of data they took into account (even if in fact they read little of it).

c *Empathetic (or relationship-based) buyers* will seek to get to know you before they do business. Any attempt to pull them away from a conversation about your family, interests, etc before they are ready will often stop them from engaging with you and ruin a sale. Play along and, in many cases, you will find that the conversation draws to a close with: 'When can we start?'

d *Cooperative (or partnership-based) buyers* will ask questions about how working together can be made a win for both parties. They want to understand not simply, 'What's in it for me?' but, 'What's in it for you?' so that they can be assured that your interests and theirs are aligned.

Once again, the benefit of understanding how the client makes buying decisions is that you can adjust the way in which you articulate the value that you bring in language that resonates, and also adjust the way in which you manage the relationship with the client as it develops. That will make it easier for the client to see that you seek to add value rather than simply to win a piece of work, assuming that is the case. If it is not and all you want is a piece of work that may be OK in the very short term. However, once you have set yourself up in that kind of role in the mind of the client it will be hard to get out of it. As a result, you will be pigeon-holed as the commodity supplier and your fees will be limited accordingly. Ultimately it will kill your business.

If you find yourself dealing with a client who thinks and operates only in transactional/commodity mode, you may feel a need to do one piece of work with them, if only to explore whether it is possible to develop the relationship further. If it proves not to be possible, it is often better to look for other opportunities rather than to repeat the transactional process, unless it is one that is profitable for you and in which you feel comfortable. This of course goes back to defining the right kind of client for you (once again we looked at this in Chapters 1 and 2).

'Learning preference' means simply how the client prefers to receive information. There are several different models to describe this. A simple but powerful model is Fleming's 'VAK' approach, which looks at three dimensions: visual, auditory and kinaesthetic:

a *Visual learners* prefer to see information in the form of pictures, graphs, etc. They will react well to visual language and images. They will ask how you see things, how they look to you, etc.

b *Auditory learners* like to listen to descriptions. The will ask how a concept sounds to you. They may not maintain eye contact even though they are clearly engaged in the conversation, in order to avoid visual distractions.

c *Kinaesthetics* like to gain (literally) hands-on experience with a new product or gadget. They are the archetypal followers of the 'graduate approach' to any new mechanical or electrical item: ie push every button and turn every knob until the item either works or breaks rather than read the instruction manual, which is of course only the manufacturer's opinion on how it works. They will ask how something feels. These individuals need to quite literally 'get comfortable' with an idea, which may require several iterations during which the kinaesthetic will shift in their chair apparently experiencing physical stress. Eventually their shoulders will drop and they will relax visibly, saying something like 'OK, I'm comfortable with that.'

If in doubt, use visual language because a visual learning preference is exhibited by a majority of people. An auditory preference is next on the list, followed by kinaesthetic, but visuals are a larger group than the other two combined. In many cases an individual will have mixed preferences with one primary and a secondary; even a tertiary preference. The benefit is to be able to adjust the language you use in outlining the value you bring to the client so that they can 'get it' most easily.

3. Planning and preparation

There is obviously a lot going on in the early stages of any meeting and especially in an initial meeting. The key is to plan each and every meeting so that you set it up for success. The benefit is to reduce so far as possible the number of variables and provide a framework that helps to keep both the client and yourself focused on the results that you agree up front at the start of the meeting.

With that in mind, Table 7.1 shows the meeting planner that I use for all meetings including phone calls and video conferences. Indeed it is even more important to plan meetings that are not to be held face-to-face. The reason is that in such meetings you lose a considerable amount of the 'para-language'

TABLE 7.1   Meeting planner

When and where:

Date	Time	Location or dial-in details

Who will attend?

Who *must* be there?		What is their role in this meeting?	
Your firm	Client firm	Your firm	Client firm

Your *actual* aim in this meeting (Note: This may not be the same as the *stated* aim):

Your *stated* aim in this meeting (the exact words that you will use to the client):

The results you wish to achieve (in the words that you will use to the client):

Result 1	
Result 2	
Result 3	

TABLE 7.1 *continued*

The questions you will ask to identify 'fit' and what drives the client:

Question 1	
Question 2	
Question 3	

such as facial expressions and even tone of voice that are degraded or eliminated by the medium used to connect the parties (phone line, internet, etc).

The *date, time and location/dial-in details* are self-explanatory. The benefit is to provide a reminder in case of need. The details of *who is to attend* are not only a reminder of the list of attendees, but also an opportunity to think through the role of each person in the meeting, including your own.

Your own *role* in this context is the role in which you seek to position yourself both with the client firm and with the individual(s) present. These may not be identical but will usually be something like 'solution provider in respect of XYZ' or 'partner in achieving ABC'. In Chapter 6 we looked at the various roles within the client firm; technician, end user, etc. In any meeting it is important to be clear in your own mind about the role of the person or people you will be with and so far as possible therefore their span of decision and the degree to which they can promote or derail your ability to win a piece of work and/or enhance your own role with the client firm.

Your *aim* in the meeting is exactly what it says: what you wish to achieve in that meeting. It may not be the same as your *stated aim* (which is the exact words you will use with the client). For example, the aim of any initial meeting is simply to achieve a basic personal connection or 'liking and hence trust'. It is unlikely that the client would agree to that as a stated aim so that will need to be different. The stated aim should always be open and non-threatening. In many cases something as simple as 'To talk about your business' will do well.

The three fields represent the specific *results* you seek to achieve from the meeting. There should be no more than three of these because more will tend to confuse the client. A good example of *results statements* for an initial meeting might be:

- I can understand what you feel are the most important results that you must achieve over the next 12–18 months and what factors may get in the way;

- in that context I can outline some of the benefits that I and my firm can deliver; and
- we can consider opportunities to work together.

The last of these may appear a little presumptuous (certainly to a British person) but don't forget that the client knows why you are there; there is probably no harm in acknowledging it and it will differentiate you from others.

The *questions* you ask to identify needs are again exactly what it says on the tin. In general, I recommend that these questions be open-ended (ie cannot be answered by a simple Yes/No) and should relate to the results you mentioned in your opening aim and results statement. For example, based on the above results statement you might ask, 'What do you feel are the factors that define the success of your business and how will you measure them?'

By the end of the initial meeting you will need to know the answers to most if not all of the following points:

- What results must the client/the client firm achieve to ensure success on a 12–18 month view?
- How will they define success for themselves personally?
- How will they measure your success if you agree to work together?
- What factors do they feel will most likely get in their way of achieving the results they seek?

The answers to those questions will need to be heard on several levels as outlined above.

Where possible I will e-mail the client before a meeting to confirm the logistics and will include my stated aim plus the results I seek to achieve. I will also ask the client to think about the answers to at least one of the questions I have prepared. That letter or e-mail can be written using information copied and pasted from your planner form.

When I enter the meeting room and the normal introductions and pouring of coffee, etc are completed, I will sit back in my chair (expecting that this signal of relaxation will be mirrored by the client) and, prefaced by the phrase, 'Before we begin ...' ask if the client has had a chance to read the e-mail I sent prior to the meeting. In most cases the answer is 'Yes'. In some cases, the client will begin to talk immediately. More often, I will simply re-state, verbally, the aim and results exactly as outlined in the pre-meeting e-mail or letter. The benefit is that the client has seen these before and they are therefore not threatening because there is no surprise.

The client will usually nod and say 'Yes'. I can then ask if they have been able to think about the question I posed. Usually, this ensures that the client begins to talk through their response; otherwise I can reprise the question. In any event, the aim is to get the client to talk as soon as possible so that

I can begin to gather information about what drives them and about the commercial fit opportunities.

If possible, try to avoid taking notes as it will tend to detract from your active listening capacity. You can do this by bringing a colleague with you whose main responsibility is to be the note taker. I have known cases where a Dictaphone was used to record the meeting with the consent of the client. However, in my view this will tend to prevent both you and the client from 'just being themselves' and hence makes the meeting less effective. Active listening and a few notes will normally suffice. So far as possible you need to be able to recall the exact words the client uses in answering your questions. This becomes important when you need to outline the value you deliver and especially if it becomes necessary to capture these ideas in the form of a confirmation letter.

Once you have begun a meeting as outlined above, and once the client begins to talk, the meeting will take on a life of its own. The aim is to gather as much information as you can before you get to the point where you outline a possible solution to the issues that the client has raised. In many cases you will not be able to solve every issue that the client raises. If that is the case, focus on those where you can help. If there are none, just say so.

Note that some of the issues you will hear raised are not solvable in themselves because the solution is in fact an outcome of success in other areas. A common issue might be a need to 'increase cash flow' or to 'increase profitability'. Both are outcomes of an increase in either customer numbers, the amount of money each customer spends on each occasion they do business, or increasing the profit margin per sale. You may be able to help in one or more of those areas, but you cannot, as such, increase cash flow or profitability.

Outlining your solution

Once you have gathered as much information as you reasonably can, there will come a point in the meeting when it is time for you to respond to the client and to outline where you feel able to help and how, plus the value you will deliver and the associated cost.

At this point it is essential that the client can visualize the benefits to themselves of your ideas. If they can, and those benefits are relevant to them in that moment, there is a strong probability that they will say 'Yes'. This presupposes that the normal conditions of personal connection or rapport and trust, budget availability and congruence of solution (ie your proposed plan looks something like what they had in mind) are in place. Too often people in the professional services field focus on what they do and how they do it rather than on the results that the client will experience. The client is not usually interested in the process (unless they are a highly informational buyer); they care only about the results and the cost/hassle equation.

With that in mind, a little more prior planning will be helpful, which can occur long before you go into any meeting. It is simply to prepare a number of generic value statements that can be adjusted as required to address the needs of a given client (which have become apparent during your initial meeting). The key is to link explicitly at least one benefit and one result for the client to each solution idea. For example:

Issue: 'Mr Client, you mention that you are not currently meeting your goals for profit per client account.'

Solution idea: 'We have a process that has been proven over a number of years to pre-select clients who are able to give you the kind of larger deals you need.'

Benefit: 'By using that approach, your people will be able to identify the right sort of clients and focus on them so they will save time and avoid wasted effort.'

Result: 'That will help you avoid the "profitless prosperity trap" where everyone is frantically busy but you make no real money.'

Ideally, the client will be able to visualize the benefits you will deliver and the results they will experience, and this combination will generate a 'When can you start?' response. In some cases, there will be an additional step, which the client may refer to as 'writing a proposal' but which should in fact be no more than confirming what has been agreed during the meeting.

Writing great proposals

Where possible, I avoid writing proposals. For many professionals, a request from the client to write a proposal is the result they seek from a meeting to 'close the business'. In my experience, if a client asks for a proposal before you have agreed on an outline solution and the approximate associated cost, that indicates either that the benefits are as yet unclear and/or that the client does not have budget available and/or the authority to commit that budget. In any event, the request for a proposal is likely to be a smokescreen and it will be necessary to ask additional questions to ascertain what the core issue is. Otherwise you will spend a lot of time on writing proposals that go nowhere. What I do write, following early meetings with a client who has agreed in principle to a given engagement, is a letter of confirmation.

Once you have agreement in principle, that letter will normally be needed only for the purpose of gaining agreement from others in the client firm; for example the rest of the board or in some cases where the engagement is large, for a technician or user to gain approval from the CEO or equivalent to proceed to a pilot engagement, following which the board can be asked to approve the larger follow up.

The keys to success in any such letter are that it passes the SLURP test; in other words it is:

Short

Lucid

Unambiguous

Realistic and

Price is linked to benefits.

That letter will follow much the same format as a meeting planner. After a short introductory paragraph ('I enjoyed our conversation'), the second paragraph is an aim and results statement for that letter. It might be as simple as: 'To confirm what we agreed in terms of the results you seek, my proposed solution plus the outline process of engagement, the benefits/results it will deliver and the associated cost.' In some cases, especially if the client needs to gain internal agreement, the letter will set up a further meeting to 'answer any questions you or your colleagues may have and agree how to proceed'.

The third paragraph of the letter starts to replay in bullet point form what the client said about their issues, the results they seek, how they will measure success and any factors that they feel may hinder them in achieving their aims.

Next comes a short outline of the solution you propose plus the benefits and results that will occur. Finally, there is a single paragraph on fees. The whole thing should be not more than two or at most three sides of A4 in length. Use short paragraphs with sub-headings and bulleted lists to break up the text, making it easier to read. Keep the sentences short without being staccato. Use simple vocabulary rather than jargon where possible.

By all means you can add appendices. Indeed for any client that may be an informational buyer, doing so is almost mandatory. If it is appropriate you can have more than one appendix; for example one on process of engagement, one with relevant case studies, one on the basis of calculation of your fee, one with terms and conditions (including such things as cancellation of scheduled meetings, etc).

The vast majority of these appendices can be pre-prepared. They will form another element in your marketing collateral. I urge you not to add a file name in the header or footer that may indicate that the material was prepared for a specific client. In a past life, I recall receiving the first presentation following the start of a new engagement with a firm of consultants. They had pitched on the basis that ours was the first large British fund manager for whom they had worked and that they would accordingly do a significant project for a far lower fee than usual, simply to add the name of our firm to their roll of clients. That presentation carried a file name in the footer with the name of another British fund management firm. Oops!

In reality few clients will read the appendices and certainly not in any detail; they serve to 'prove that you have done the work', however. As the information is presented in the form of appendices, it does not risk possible confusion nor of overwhelming the client as it might if presented as part of the letter.

By preparing a letter confirming the conversation, you are sending a signal that the deal is already agreed in principle. By replaying to the client their own definition of the issues to be addressed and linking directly the benefits of your solution and the results that the client will experience, you make it harder for the client to say 'No'; indeed if the benefits and results are clear, the only issues can be process and price. The letter should make it clear that the solution proposed is a recommendation but that it is subject to adjustment if the client requires it.

As for the price, I recommend asking the client quite early in the conversation what budget is available to enable the issues they have identified to be resolved. If the client is coy, I resist offering a price on the grounds that there may be several options and I cannot determine which is feasible unless I have an idea of budget availability. I frequently emphasize to new potential clients that I do not willingly lose business on the basis of price alone, so we need to have an adult conversation to balance the desired results, the process of engagement and the cost both in cash and time for both parties. If at all possible, I prefer to work on the basis of a flat, all-inclusive retainer fee.

Powerful PowerPoints®

Once again, I try not to use PowerPoint® presentation decks. The reason is that I find they get in the way of the process of conversation. If I feel a need to prepare one I will try to avoid using it in a meeting (for the same reason) but may use it as a leave-behind. This can be especially useful if a client has previously indicated that they will need to consult colleagues; I will then be giving the client the right ammunition to ensure that their colleagues are most likely to say 'Yes'.

A good PowerPoint® deck is one that, like a good proposal or letter of confirmation, will pass the 'SLURP' test outlined above. Far too many decks contain way too much information and too many slides. There is a considerable body of research from the world of psychology that indicates that the human brain can hold only a limited number (usually summarized as 7 +/− 2) of items of information in working memory at any given time. One of the earliest and most commonly-cited pieces of research on the subject was carried out by George A Miller of Princeton University in 1956. His '7 +/− 2' result is referred to as 'Miller's Law'. More recent research indicates that the actual number may in fact be lower (three or four).

With that in mind, the maximum number of slides in a PowerPoint® deck should be nine, although that does not prevent the addition of as many slides as you wish in the form of appendices (once again, sheer volume of data may be necessary to convince certain types of client that you have 'done the work'). Appendices can also be helpful for use as reference points in answering questions, although you will need to know your way around the deck to use them effectively.

The detail content of the deck will depend on the stage you have reached in developing the relationship with the client on the project under consideration. In an initial meeting, it can be tempting to arrive with a deck through which you can talk because it will structure the process. This almost inevitably leads to an 'information dump' and usually gets in the way of the success of the 'inverted' meeting process outlined above. I very rarely bring a deck to an initial meeting; just a copy of my pre-meeting e-mail or letter in case the client has not received or read it.

Each slide in your deck should contain enough information to convey a specific point that is relevant to the client. A client should be able to read the slide and understand the point being made within 5 seconds or less. It is always a mistake to try to hide one section of a slide in order to make points sequentially. To avoid exceeding the client's working memory limit, I avoid the use of 'builds' in a slide where each new point is added on a new slide.

Where possible avoid copying detailed data such as a spreadsheet into a PowerPoint® slide as it will become hard to read, especially if projected onto a screen. Pick out the salient points and present them in graphic form if possible. Be wary of the use of colour. Around 10 per cent of humanity has a problem of some kind with colour perception; the most common being the ability to distinguish between red and green. Avoid coloured backgrounds for the same reason. In some cases the use of colour will be perceived to be environmentally unfriendly as it will use more resources if the deck is printed.

You should usually open with a stated aim and results slide that relates to the meeting at which you will use the deck or after which it will form a 'leave-behind'. If you have had the chance to ask questions to identify the specific needs of the client you can reprise these in a second slide (or perhaps in two further slides if you need to outline some background data or describe the commercial fit you have identified). The next part of the deck can outline your solution (one or two slides) and the benefits/results for the client (a further one to three slides). The final slide should be a call to action or 'next steps' proposal.

By this point, we should be well on the way to winning business from clients that match closely the definition we came up with earlier of a 'perfect' client. In the next chapter we explore what needs to be done when the client does indeed say 'Yes' and you get into the process of delivery.

Managing your delivery and the client's expectations

08

So far we have looked at how to maximize the probability that you come out of a meeting with a prospective client that you want to work with having heard the magic words 'OK. When can you start?' In this chapter we examine how you manage the delivery process thereafter in such a way that you move your relationship with the client yet further up the relationship pyramid – or keep it at the partnership level if it is already there.

In that context, we explore how to go about quality assurance (QA) and its importance even if you are a 'solo-preneur'. We look at how to manage the separate elements of project delivery, client ownership and management of the relationship. We examine the use of after-action reports, internal and external feedback loops, milestone management and the development of a 'no surprises' culture. The latter stops you and the client from being blindsided by events that could (and therefore should) have been foresee-able. We also look at pulling the plug on a project and knowing when that is the right thing to do (and when to advise the client that it is the right thing to do).

Getting all of the above at least approximately right helps to cement your long-term relationship with each client and also maximizes the probability that you will be able to gain excellent referrals from all of them (something we look at in detail in Chapter 9). All of the above must also be made to support your personal brand and your business brand; it is about ensuring congruence of delivery with your brand and hence its authenticity.

Quality assurance (QA)

QA is something that many professionals, especially those in small firms or who are solo-preneurs, take for granted; they assume it is not something on which they need to focus immediately when they take on a piece of work. They also assume that, unless the client says, 'Hey; there's a problem' all is going well and that the client is delighted with both what is being delivered and how it is delivered. In my experience, assumption is in this instance, as is usually the case, the mother of all errors.

Unless something is going dramatically wrong, few clients will voice concerns unless asked specifically for feedback. If they have to wait to be asked, the feedback may well be far more negative than would have been the case had it been sought actively, routinely and early. If clients have low-level concerns, the fact that they are not asked for feedback is likely to drive the real level of your relationship at least one level down the relationship pyramid. That in turn opens or increases the possibility of being supplanted by a competitor. Don't forget that a competitor may appear in the form of either 'Do nothing' or 'Use in-house resources' as well as someone else who is active in your field.

Whether you are a solo-preneur or a member of a large firm, it is important both to plan and to carry out QA actively during any project on which you are working. Your QA process begins before you start work on a given project, by defining clearly not only what results must be delivered as a result of your work but how the client will judge your success. That in turn goes right back to the answers given to the questions you ask in your initial meeting to identify the specific commercial needs and what drives the client (how they take decisions, etc).

In writing your letter confirming to the client what you have agreed to deliver and an outline of the process, resources needed etc, you may not have set out specific milestones or checkpoints for your work. It is a good idea to do so at an early stage in the project and ideally before you actually begin work. You can call the document your 'Outline project plan' or 'Milestones' or whatever makes sense for this piece of work. The benefit is to set expectations not only about your delivery and timings but also about what resources may be needed from the client's side. It will allow the client an opportunity to tell you that they prefer to follow a different approach.

Your milestones document need not be set out in exhaustive detail unless the client is a highly informational buyer. In most cases it will be quite sufficient to capture:

- date due for a given action;
- result to be achieved as at that date;
- measurement factors.

You may wish to add who is responsible for the delivery of that element of the project if it is not yourself and who else is involved where appropriate. (Typically this is only necessary in larger or more complex projects where there are several streams of work occurring in parallel.) The milestones document can be used as your own project plan in the case of relatively simple projects, where it can be used as a tactical checklist to ensure that nothing drops through the cracks.

Having set milestones, you can then plan backwards from the due date of each element to ensure that you have allowed enough time and the necessary resources to achieve the result required. Where possible, as you approach a milestone or immediately afterwards, have a conversation with the relevant person within the client firm (it may be the user or the technician rather than the primary buyer) to ensure that they are happy with what has been achieved and that it meets the success criteria that have been agreed. Deal immediately with any concerns that may be raised. Once any outstanding issues or concerns are resolved, make sure that the primary buyer is informed that things are on track and that the relevant milestone has been passed successfully.

If it becomes clear that a milestone may not be achievable, let the relevant person and the primary buyer within the client firm know at once. Present the problem in outline and how you will resolve it, as well as communicating any consequent delay, not only to that part of the project but also to the project as a whole. If there is a financial consequence, make sure that that is highlighted. It is far better to flag a potential issue and resolve it than to keep quiet, allowing the client to believe that all is well until the last moment.

No client likes a surprise – not even what you may assume is a pleasant one such as an underspend on budget. If you know that you will bring in a project under budget, tell the client as soon as possible so that they can reallocate the cash if they wish. An unexpected end of project 'gift' that cannot at that point be redirected is almost as bad as running over budget without agreement.

This sort of complexity is one of the reasons why I prefer to agree a flat fee for a given project at the outset and also a fixed timeframe. Not only does it obviate any issue of budget over-run, it also reinforces discipline and rigour on my part in ensuring that I understand the requirements of the project, that it is effectively planned and that the plans are realistic. It also means that I need to have a very clear idea of my costs to deliver a project. I very rarely find that a client will ask for a daily rate as opposed to a flat fee, especially if the fee includes expenses. In the rare event that a project over-runs in terms of time, it is far easier to ask for a few days grace if those days are not directly chargeable to the client.

In theory this approach could be risky for me. If I underestimate the time and other resources needed to achieve the agreed results, I may find that a project is unprofitable or indeed that I lose money. In reality, I find that, so long as the desired results are clear and realistic and I am also realistic about costs (in fact I keep my delivery costs very lean), it is highly profitable overall, in the vast majority of cases. It also obviates any need for time to be wasted, by me or by the client, on discussions over expenses such as air travel and hotel bills. As long as I turn up as planned the client need not know and almost certainly does not care whether I flew economy or business class and whether I bought the ticket using cash or frequent-flyer miles.

QA is not just about delivery on time and on budget. It is also about delivery in a manner that meets and if possible exceeds the client's expectations. It is for that reason that it is so important to determine at the outset how the client will judge your success: what are the factors involved and how will you be measured. What may seem to you to be a minor issue may be of importance to the client.

In a past corporate role of mine, it was deemed to be a serious failing if spelling or grammatical errors were found in a document that had gone out to a client, so much so that every such document had to be read and counter-signed by someone of equivalent or higher seniority to the person signing it. The counter-signatory also had to be familiar with the subject matter and was held to be equally responsible for any error that might subsequently be found. That might appear to be unduly harsh. However, that approach picked up an error in a contract that showed the annual management fee for a multi-million pound investment agreement incorrectly; the decimal point was one place out, which could have cost the firm 90 per cent of the agreed fee. It also picked up the fact that another contract showed the heading 'Terms and Conditions' with the letters 'nd' missing, making the heading 'Terms and Coitions'. It was more embarrassing than it might appear as the contract was with a religious foundation.

QA goes even beyond exceeding the client's expectations. It is the means by which you reinforce and enhance your brand, personally and as a business. It is the means by which you evidence in your business your own personal values and behaviours. What the client experiences in working with you should be completely congruent with what they would experience in spending time with you socially or, more important, in a situation involving some form of stress, whether that is taking part in a sporting event or spending a few days walking in the wilderness. When you cooperate with the client to enable them to win a new piece of business, they should feel confident that they can rely on you under stress or in adversity.

Simply 'doing the right thing' is a good start; a necessary but not sufficient attribute to locking in a partnership relationship with the client. It is not quite the same as 'doing the right thing no matter how hard it gets'. That reinforces the T of the initial L+T to the extent that you reinforce your partnership status and lock out competitors – at least so long as you continue to deliver that same experience to the client.

Delivery, client ownership and CRM

We have so far focused mainly on delivery in the context of QA. Delivery is not usually static in any client engagement or project, but dynamic. That is because in most cases the process of delivery will throw up glitches that demand a change to the plan at a tactical level. In some cases the glitch may be sufficient to cause a strategic rethink.

As an example, a client of mine who had begun to produce a range of gifts using screen-printed linen under a certain trade name arrived in her office to find a 'cease and desist' letter from a firm of lawyers regarding a breach of trademark rights. It appeared that she had failed to check properly whether the proposed name of her business might breach a trademark even though it was not shown as a company name on the UK Companies House list. That could have been a disaster for her for all the obvious reasons. In the event, she was able to change the name of her business to her own, register the relevant domain name in both .com and .co.uk formats and gain agreement to sell off the stock she had on hand at the time without altering the name shown on each article. She had to change the name on her company bank account and amend the name of the company itself. However, these were minor issues. Thankfully, the problem came to light early on before the business was fully established, otherwise it could have cost her months of work developing her brand and making it known to clients, only to be forced into a name change.

Delivery in a professional services context should ideally be 'business as usual'; it is simply doing what you do and more specifically what you have undertaken to do for a given client. However, you should expect that the deliverables may change as you get into a project – almost regardless of relative size and complexity. You will need to have flexibility built into your plans to allow for this. There are two potential areas of impact as a result: resourcing (including time available), and hence the second: fees.

To be absolutely clear, change is the only constant in business. It would be foolhardy to expect any project to proceed according to plan and without speed bumps or barriers. Indeed, General Eisenhower is reputed to have said that plans are in themselves useless as they never survive contact with reality (or in his context, with the enemy). However, the process of planning is essential. Delivery, then, is not simply about 'getting through' a project and making sure that the outcomes you agreed at the outset are achieved; it is about gaining and retaining control over multiple moving pieces.

If the changes that you encounter to a given piece of work are tactical rather than strategic, it is almost always preferable simply to accept and accommodate those changes and move on with delivery of the required results for the client. If the changes to the project are strategic – in other words if they alter the end results – you may need a rethink. In either case, involve the client in the decision process rather than presenting them with a fait accompli.

Clearly, if your fees are set on a daily rate basis, strategic changes to the results that are to be delivered may give rise to a conversation with the client about additional cost, which can damage the relationship unless it is handled sensitively. Within reason, it is usually far better for the relationship to stick to your original quoted fee and absorb any additional time needed for delivery. If your fee is quoted on a flat 'rate for the job' basis, it is usually easier to build in flexibility in delivery. Your focus is, like the client's, on outputs not inputs (results, not time spent).

This sort of conversation is easier to manage well if the roles of delivery, client ownership and client relationship management are distinct and separate. For example, in my corporate past in the investment management industry, each client had three points of contact with the firm: their fund manager, the fund administrator and the client director. The fund manager was responsible for day-to-day investment of the money. The fund administrator ensured that performance measurement and reporting were done accurately and in a timely manner as well as ensuring that any restrictions on investment were taken into account. The client director had overall responsibility for (ie 'owned') the relationship between the client and the investment management firm. If there was either good news or bad news, the client director was responsible for its communication.

If your firm has the resources available, this is not a bad model to follow. It helps to ensure that QA is visible to the client and provides opportunities to extend your firm's surface area with the client firm. However, it is vital to ensure that your own internal communication is excellent in order to avoid the common problem of 'left hand and right hand' perceived not to be aware of what each other is doing.

Client ownership is arguably the glue that binds delivery and CRM (customer relationship management). If it is possible to have a senior person within your firm positioned as having overall responsibility for the relationship with a given client, it can help to defuse tactical friction at the coalface of a project. It also facilitates extending the surface area of your firm within the client firm so that you are in a better position to win internal referrals and indeed additional business elsewhere where there is no issue of conflict of interest. If it is not practicable to separate the roles of client owner, CRM and delivery, it is usually best to position the ownership of the relationship with the client as part of CRM.

'Client relationship management' is a term that is often associated with complex computer systems and databases. In its simplest and most effective form, it is no more than common sense put into practice. What does CRM mean in this context? It includes:

- Keeping all of the relevant buyers on the client's side informed of progress against plan.

- Where necessary, ensuring that each of these buyers is consulted. That might include ensuring that necessary resources from the client firm's side are in fact available when you need them or making alternative arrangements if not.

- Managing expectations.

- Ensuring that resources provided by the client firm will be available as planned and will arrive with you properly committed.

- Pre-positioning any information that is to be presented at meetings such as steering committees. The benefit is that such meetings take far less time, the decision-making process is shorter and less fraught with stress, and the probability that you will gain the decisions you need is greatly increased.

- When appropriate, planting the seeds of future referrals both within the client firm and externally (we look at referrals in more detail in Chapter 9).

If you are part of a larger firm (or one that has more than a handful of employees), it is reasonably easy to create CRM as a role that is separate from delivery and as a discipline in its own right. However, I would argue that it is something of which every member of your firm should be aware and for which they should take personal responsibility. As such, an awareness of CRM needs to form part of the development plan for every member of staff in your firm, regardless of seniority or whether their role is deemed to be 'client facing'. (The number of calls that find their way to technicians in your finance or administration areas will no doubt be surprising.)

As a small firm or solo-preneur, CRM is inextricably linked to your day-to-day work; it must be treated as such and must have time allocated. Out of every project, I expect to spend between 10 and 20 per cent of the overall elapsed time on CRM matters for the client with whom I am working at that moment. The higher level reflects the time taken to QA the work done by any associates that I may use on a project in addition to day-to-day project management.

In a typical month, I expect to spend at least 80 per cent of my time that is not taken up with actual delivery of work with clients on a combination of CRM (ie follow-up with existing clients), marketing and sales activity. The remainder will be allocated to business administration (<5 per cent; I outsource as much as practicable), my own CPD (c7.5 per cent, excluding routine reading) and planning (c7.5 per cent).

A key part of effective CRM is record keeping. This is not to say that a complex computer system is needed to keep those records. In fact, the simpler the system, the more likely it is to be used. It is of course quite possible to have an effective CRM *process* without an actual CRM *system*. However, that is usually feasible only for very small businesses or solo-preneurs. Where more than one person is likely to interact with a given client or client firm it saves you from possible embarrassment if you all use the same system and have access to the same data.

Ideally your CRM system and your e-mail system, plus your office 'productivity' software (eg MS Word®, Excel®) will be linked so that it is easy to track interactions with any client. There are numerous CRM software packages available for businesses of all sizes. These range from MS Outlook® with Business Contact Manager through software such as ACT® by Sage, Cloud-based solutions like Salesforce.com to full-blown Oracle systems.

There is in my experience no one 'right' solution for any given business. Leaving aside cost and the number of client contacts to be tracked, much will depend on the level of technical knowledge of your staff: the simpler the system is to use, the more likely it is that those who are not digital natives will use it. More important, if your CRM system is integrated in the way you do business to the extent that keeping the records up to date is just a by-product of what you do anyway, it is far more likely that the system will remain up to date and hence be used: nothing drops out of use so fast as a system that is seen to be out of date.

Ideally, for example, the act of sending out an e-mail to a client should be logged on your CRM system. Similarly, your telephone system can be linked to the CRM system so that the fact you made the call is noted. You may need to add notes of the content manually; something that is essentially just good practice. Once you have a CRM system integrated into your business processes in this way, it allows you to plan your follow-ups to both clients and prospective clients so that you always know where you are (or where you should be). This does of course beg the question of data control and backup, which we explore in Chapter 10.

After-action reports and feedback loops

Every interaction with a client or potential client should be looked upon as a learning opportunity. The benefit is to make sure that as little as possible is left to chance in developing and maintaining the relationship. It is also helpful in ensuring that, if you fall ill, someone else in your firm can pick up the reins with minimal disturbance. After action reports (AARs) and feedback loops serve a similar purpose in that they help you to learn from each client interaction. However, they differ in approach.

AAR is a term borrowed from the military where each contact with the enemy is reviewed to find out what was learnt about the enemy, what could have been done differently, etc. In the professional services context, I recommend treating each meeting and each piece of delivery for a client as something that should be the subject of an AAR. As ever, it is more likely that an AAR will be completed if the process is simplified as much as possible. I use the template shown in Table 8.1 to capture the key data. Once the AAR has been reviewed it should go into your CRM system so that, over time, you build up a picture of your interactions with the client and can begin to extrapolate from that information when it comes to planning.

As you will see, much of the information in the AAR can be copied directly from your initial meeting plan document; another benefit of completing one for each meeting. The key additions are the 'Next steps' and the two final fields: what went well and what could have been done differently or better.

The 'Next steps' information should of course be fed back to the client to confirm what has been agreed. There is little point in recording a next step unless it has an attached 'due by' data and the name of the person responsible. These two items help to enforce accountability. However, it is not good practice in my view to assign responsibility for a next step to someone who was not present (or at least represented) at the meeting.

The real learning aspect of an AAR lies in the fields 'What went well?' and 'What could have been done differently or better?' It is always better for morale to think first of what went well and it tends to be easier to reinforce those behaviours or actions if they are considered first. Rather than looking at 'What went wrong', it is easier for people to look at what could have been done differently; their responses will tend to be less defensive and this approach tends to depersonalize the problem if there is one so that it is easier to have an objective discussion about solutions and future prevention.

The concept of the feedback loop is less formal but equally powerful; see Figure 8.1. It operates both internally within your own firm, externally between your firm and the client and (ideally) internally within the client firm.

A feedback loop aims to open a channel of communication that is usually informal and ensures that all of the relevant people are encouraged to use it actively and constructively to enhance the overall experience of working together to achieve mutually understood aims.

A feedback loop is essentially two-way. That means that it allows you to give feedback to the client as well to receive it from the client. It allows you to give feedback to colleagues and to receive it from them. The feedback loop must be open at all times, transparent and honest. There need be no specific time for feedback to be given or received. (That said, it is often helpful to remind clients and colleagues periodically that feedback is actively sought.) There can be no 'off the record' conversations. If feedback refers to an individual or group they must be made aware of it and have an opportunity to discuss it so that they can both learn from it and correct any misunderstandings that may have occurred.

TABLE 8.1   After Action Report template

Date of meeting / call				
Who was involved?	Client:		Our team:	
Aim of meeting				
Desired results	1			
	2			
	3			
Questions we asked	1			
	2			
	3			
Answers we received	1			
	2			
	3			
Agreed next steps/ Who is responsible? / By when?			Who?	When?
	1			
	2			
	3			
What went well?				
What could have been done differently or better?				

FIGURE 8.1   Feedback loops

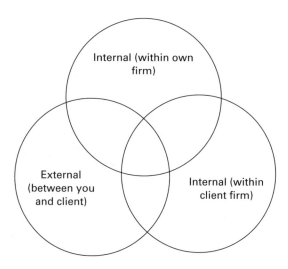

Feedback can be verbal or written. If it is verbal, it is essential to record the content at least in summary form (it goes into the CRM system). If feedback is not recorded, the benefit degrades in direct proportion to the half-life of individual and corporate memory, which can be remarkably short.

Feedback loops can be used not only in the context of project-type work with a client; they are also invaluable as an ongoing evaluation of performance within your own firm. Sadly, too many professional services firms still rely on an outdated approach to performance evaluation so that it is an 'annual appraisal' rather than dynamic and continual encouragement and guidance. In this context, it is of tremendous benefit to ensure that the feedback operates two-way; it increases the engagement of staff, tends to improve communication overall and allows individuals who may be quite junior in the hierarchy to act autonomously in full knowledge of your strategic aims.

The benefit for you is to reduce significantly the amount of time and effort needed for hands-on management. You can instead focus on leading your team by setting strategic aims, ensuring that individuals have the necessary skills and knowledge to achieve them, and then simply standing out of their way while monitoring what is going on in order to ensure that no balls are dropped – or if they are that they can be retrieved.

Milestones

In any piece of work undertaken in the professional services industry, there will be milestones. In a very simple project there may be only one: actual delivery of what has been agreed. More commonly, there will be many milestones marking the progress of the project towards completion, both in terms of timing of delivery and (often) how 'delivery' is to be measured. In a complex project, with several streams of work occurring in parallel, milestones may also represent dependencies ('We can't start XYZ until ABC is completed'). Milestones can therefore become a way to break down and plan the project and also to measure the quality of the results achieved.

Milestones represent opportunities to communicate with the client and with colleagues and are a way to maintain focus or avoid 'project creep' where items are added – sometimes surreptitiously – to the agreed delivery. They are an opportunity to manage expectations and to flag possible problems. By monitoring progress against agreed milestones, you (or the person who 'owns' the client relationship) can also manage resourcing from both sides and pre-position both progress reports and decisions that must be made prior to any formal meeting such as a steering committee.

In managing a piece of work, it is important to review progress against milestones in good time prior to the milestone date. If there is a problem, you then have time to take action to resolve it and/or to manage the expectations of the client and your own colleagues. This is the basis of a 'no surprises' culture and can be helped enormously by the use of your feedback loops. The aim is that nobody should feel scared of delivering 'bad news' and that messengers who bring bad news will be praised rather than shot. This in turn reinforces the feeling of all involved in a project that, regardless of seniority, they are empowered and enabled to be successful, which in turn reinforces engagement and loyalty.

Pulling the plug

It shouldn't happen, but it almost certainly will. Despite all your best efforts there is likely to come a time when a project in which you are involved, or where you own the client relationship, is objectively failing. Alternatively, a project may no longer be viable due to changed circumstances or market conditions. For whatever reason, it appears to be time to pull the plug. Clearly both you and the client will have done everything you can to avoid this situation and your use of feedback loops and AARs will have helped to avoid this coming as a surprise to either side. When it occurs, the most important questions are how to recognize the situation and how to handle it.

The key alarm signal for which to be alert is change; change of personnel, change of the client firm's market position (for example it becomes an acquisition target or begins to seek an acquisition) or change of the results that the client wishes to achieve as a result of your work. There are some obvious indicators of problems such as continual failure to achieve milestones, despite your best efforts, meaning that the project begins to run increasingly behind schedule. Others that may be less obvious include any significant change in resourcing (for example diversion of key people to other projects) or changes of personnel, especially at a senior level on the client side.

If your primary buyer is promoted, transferred to another role within the firm or simply leaves for example, you should expect that your project will be reviewed and that in turn may indicate that it will be altered or ended. It may as a result of a review be changed to the extent that you can no longer deliver the desired results or at least not within the budget that has been set. If internal resources that had been allocated to your project by the client are withdrawn or become less available than planned, that will impact your ability to deliver.

If your resourcing has been arbitrarily reduced by 30 per cent for example, that means one of two things: the timeframe for delivery must be extended by a similar amount (or the scope reduced) or the project must be stopped and put on ice at least for the time being. If the timeframe is to be extended and if you have agreed a flat fee for delivery of the project, you may need to renegotiate your fees. Alternatively, you might flex the plan so that you need not be involved full time and can slot in other work alongside.

If none of these can be achieved you will need to absorb the additional cost or walk away. The latter is of course a nuclear option and it is one I have, to date, never had to use. It is of course helpful to link your deliverables and your fees to the availability of resources from the client side if they are required and to cover in your agreement the possibility of adding further resources from your firm at an additional cost to the client.

Questions to identify whether the project remains viable include:

- Are the agreed end results still relevant to the overall strategic success of the client?
- Can I and my team still deliver them in current circumstances?
- Are those results still achievable within the constraints of budget and available resources?
- In the new circumstances that now obtain, does the project still deliver the benefits to the client that made it attractive in the first instance?
- To the extent that there has been a change of client personnel (especially at primary buyer level) does this project touch the same emotional 'decision hot buttons' with the new players? If not, can the way in which the benefits are articulated be altered to do so?
- Who in the client firm does this project now benefit directly or indirectly? Will its success make them look good in the eyes of their senior colleagues? If it is seen to be a failure will it damage them in any way? Could its failure be presented by them as a hang-over from the 'old regime'?

- Is either the budget or the resourcing flexible in any way?
- Can the delivery timeframe be altered?
- What factors are blocking the delivery of the required results? Can these be overcome?

Depending on the answers to these questions, the first step in handling the situation is of course to have a 'grown-up' conversation with the primary buyer (probably pre-positioned via your technicians and user buyers) to highlight the issues and talk about a way forward. The key to success in such conversations is to grasp reality by the throat rather than trying to fudge the situation. If the primary buyer has changed, you should expect to reprise the entire initial sale and engagement process – even though the elapsed time may be far shorter than before and you may well be able to benefit from direct experience of working with the client firm so that you are more aware of potential internal political land-mines.

If it becomes necessary to pull the plug on a project, it is in my experience better that you raise the issue with the client than vice versa. It is also better for you to highlight the problems that will prevent delivery or make the project no longer viable or relevant and, where appropriate, to offer alternatives. That approach will tend to reinforce your role as a business partner rather than as a commercial supplier and in turn will make it more likely that the relationship will remain intact even if this piece of work is declared dead. You will therefore survive this setback and be able to re-engage with this client from a position of relative strength.

Disappointment is a powerful emotion. It is all the more powerful and damaging to your relationship if the client finds out about a problem from someone other than you. It may be tempting to avoid bringing bad news, especially to a 'difficult' client. The consequences of being anything other than proactive in doing so are negative. If you allow a client relationship to be damaged, it will impact not only the perceived success of your current project but also the likelihood of winning additional work and of gaining referrals, which are the life blood of any professional services business.

In the next chapter we look at the power of great referrals, how to go about winning them to secure repeat business and additional business and at the mechanics of what is usually called 'strategic account management' (I prefer the term 'leadership' to 'management' in this context). We also look in more detail at your overall follow-up process – how you maintain contact with clients and prospective clients and link these functions into your CRM system.

Winning referrals and repeat business

09

Repeat business and referrals are the life-blood of any professional service firm. They are inextricably linked and represent a key part of what is commonly called 'strategic account management'. Few firms or individuals are fully effective in managing the process of generating either of them. In this chapter we explore how to maximize your success in this hugely important area, so that you avoid the need constantly to 'hunt and kill' new business and can instead become a good shepherd if not a farmer. The result is to eliminate the common 'feast or famine' situation in revenue terms.

It is often said that the cost (whether measured in time, cash or opportunity cost), of finding a new client and winning business from them is roughly seven times greater than that of winning additional business from an existing client. In my experience, that is probably an underestimate unless the new potential client comes as a result of a referral, in which case the process will usually be short-circuited somewhat. If you are seeking to win business as a professional by way of untargeted direct marketing or cold calling, it is likely that you will find new clients thin on the ground and indeed you will come across them more by luck than judgement.

If I look back over the first 10 years of running my own business, I find it hard to think of a single client that did not come to me by way of a referral, whether directly or indirectly. Each referral arose largely because I asked for it. The person who gave the referral was able to do so because I could outline exactly what I was looking for and the benefits I could deliver to such a client. With the majority of those new clients, I was able to use internal referrals to extend my surface area within the client firm to win additional or repeat business.

In this chapter we explore how that process works for me and also how to develop a system for what is normally called 'strategic account management' but which I prefer to think of as 'strategic account leadership'. The principles apply equally to businesses of all sizes. However, the implementation will differ somewhat depending on the size and nature of your own firm. If you are able to build an effective strategic account leadership approach for your business, it will help to smooth out what would otherwise be a common problem of 'sine wave income flows' – otherwise known as feast or famine.

Five referral errors – and how to avoid them

In my experience the following five errors get in the way of winning referrals:

1 Not defining clearly what a great referral would look like for you (or, putting it another way, to whom you can deliver greatest value).

2 Failure to state clearly the value you deliver (as opposed to what you do).

3 Confusing an introduction with a referral.

4 Not helping the person making the referral to set up the appropriate role in the mind of the potential client before you make contact.

5 Not asking for a referral at all but 'assuming' that one will be given.

For many professionals, the nearest that they get to asking for a referral is along the lines of, 'Is there anyone else here you think I should talk to?' That is of course better than not asking at all. However, it limits the question in the mind of the client to considering 'more of the same'. In other words, the client will tend to focus on the piece of work you have just done with them and (if they think about onward referral at all) whether there may be additional, similar opportunities elsewhere in their firm or (perhaps) in other firms where there is no conflict of interest. The result is to narrow your scope of activity, perhaps to a field which is not in fact your core expertise nor what you most enjoy doing.

To maximize your success in securing referrals that work most effectively for you, it is necessary to go all the way back to the definition of the 'perfect client' that we considered in Chapter 2. It is often said that managers recruit in their own image – people who are like themselves. Clients tend to give referrals in the same way. Indeed great clients tend to give great referrals. By the same token I would try to avoid referrals from 'poor' clients: there is indeed such a thing as a bad referral. However, the great clients may not always recognize in themselves the characteristics that make them a 'perfect client' in your eyes.

To ensure that they understand fully what a great referral looks like for you, it is necessary to tell them explicitly what sort of individual you are looking for in an ideal world, both in terms of characteristics and their role. You will also need to outline what you believe to be a key challenge for such a person and the benefits you will deliver in resolving it.

This is essentially a variant on the way in which you would answer the 'first killer question' – 'What do you do?' Rather than saying something like, 'I enable self-motivated entrepreneurs to ...' by way of a self-introduction or an answer to the 'What do you do?' question, the approach in this case is more like: 'I am keen to meet self-motivated entrepreneurs who ...'. In both cases, you combine an outline description of your perfect client with a likely core issue that such individuals experience or a dream they wish to fulfil.

The next step is to add one or two of the key benefits you deliver to these people and hence to set up the role you seek with them. The key is of course to talk in terms of the value you deliver, not the process or how you do it, nor even your profession. A potential client may not be thinking in terms of hiring (for example) a consultant but about how to achieve a given result; they care only about the result. It may well be immaterial whether the person who enables them to do that is a consultant or a coach. Remember, once again, that we need to look at value through the eyes of the client who may well not see benefit in terms of cash, be it increased profit or cost reduction.

In many cases both professionals and those from whom they seek referrals confuse a referral with an introduction. An introduction is essentially social: 'Fred, this is Susan. Susan's daughter is applying for a place at Cambridge to read Economics. That was your subject, wasn't it, Fred?' By contrast, a referral is a purposeful introduction with a view to connecting individuals where there is a real and defined opportunity for a commercial fit. A referral not only effects the introduction and offers some conversational hooks (as above) but also highlights the commercial fit opportunity, the kind of benefit that the person being referred can deliver and the role they seek with a perfect client.

A referral will also include either a 'call to action' (asking the recipient to do something such as make a phone call) or to be prepared to receive and react positively to an approach such as a phone call to set up a short initial meeting. The latter is usually far more effective. A really good referral will also include a copy to the relevant EA/PA who will then be primed to put through the call (or indeed simply to schedule the meeting) rather than block it. You will normally need to make sure that each of these points is covered once the referral has been agreed in principle.

The word choice of the referral may be deliberately light-hearted but the reason why the individuals should meet will be clear to both parties. No matter how strong the relationship you have with the person making a referral on your behalf, it is important that they position you in the role that you seek with the person to whom you are being referred. That may well not be the same as the role that you have with the person making the referral, especially if your relationship with them has lasted for some time. The reason is that all relationships develop and change over time, including your professional role with the individual. With one senior partner in a law firm, I began as the person who could enable him to deliver successful integration post-merger but over time became 'the one person I can trust to tell me who's lying to me and why'. You will therefore need to tell the person making the referral how you would like to be positioned and why: even to the point of drafting a referral for them (and suggesting that it is copied to the relevant EA/PA).

It is often the case that professionals fail to ask for referrals. They simply assume that, if the client is delighted and knows of someone else who might gain similar benefits, they will make the connection. That rarely if ever occurs, in my experience. If you want referrals, you must ask for them, explicitly.

When to ask for referrals? In the case of current clients, I suggest at least twice: at the start of a project and at the end (assuming that you have delivered the results you promised). If you are involved in an extended or complex project, you can also usefully ask for referrals at appropriate milestones, especially if you can relate what has been delivered at that milestone to an aspect of your expertise that sets up a slightly different role. In other words, there are likely to be many different roles that you can fill and you can adjust the nature of the referral for which you ask according to the situation.

In the case of people you meet in the normal course of business development, networking, etc, once it becomes clear that there is no commercial fit for you with a given person there is nothing to lose by asking for a referral – or at least an introduction. I would tend not to do so immediately, however, but only after an initial meeting where, a) you have clearly established a basic personal connection even if there is no obvious business opportunity, b) you are able to describe clearly and succinctly what a good referral/introduction would look like for you and, c) it appears likely that this individual may be in a position to make such an introduction.

Internal versus external referrals

An internal referral will be within a given client firm (perhaps to someone in another division or to another geographic location). An external referral will be to someone in a different firm and who may well work in a different field. In either case it is important to avoid any possible conflict of interest and to be sensitive to internal politics.

If you are a coach working with a CEO, for example, there may be benefits that you could deliver by extending your work to that person's executive team. However, it is quite likely that the CEO may not wish you to do so. That may be to do with perceived confidentiality issues but it is also quite possible that they will simply 'not want to share their toys' with others. In that kind of case, there may be an opportunity for you to make a referral to a colleague, which is something that I highly recommend you offer. The benefit is to broaden (indirectly) your surface area within the client firm and to enhance your profile both with the client and within your own firm.

Repeat business

Repeat business may be as simple as doing the same piece of work (or a variant of it) on a regular basis – for example a coach running a team offsite event on an annual basis. It can be more complex such as undertaking a similar piece of work in other parts of a client firm, having regard to variations of culture, regulatory environment, etc.

Whatever form it may take, repeat work is similar to an internal referral in that you must ask for it: clients will rarely if ever, in my experience, automatically connect what you have recently delivered with an imminent and similar need. In some cases (for example where you are a coach who has worked with one or two members of the board) it may simply be impolitic to engage you to work with others.

In any event, once you have won a piece of work for a given client or client firm, it is incumbent on you to seek additional and/or repeat work. You will also need to plan how to maintain contact with the various buyers you already know in that firm so that you can maintain your relationship and not suffer the common problem of relationship degradation over time. Most professional relationships that are not at the level of true partnership have a half-life measured in weeks rather than years.

It is a mistake to rely too much on repeat business. Change is endemic in business and it is unusual in the professional services arena for there to be a need to do the same work more than once. Engagements will usually change over time and indeed most engagements will change as they take place and as new information and ideas come to light. Therefore, although you can and should always seek repeat business where possible, to seek referrals is likely to be more valuable over time.

Planning and process

The process of seeking referrals and repeat business is closely linked with that of building and maintaining your professional network. It differs mainly in that the reason for making contact is not, for example, to let the client have a copy of an article you have written for the trade press. I feel that it is also unlikely that you will wish to ask for a referral or repeat business other than in the context of a face-to-face meeting or during a phone conversation.

The process of seeking referrals needs to be planned in much the same manner as network development and maintenance, which we explored in Chapter 3. The frequency and nature of contact will obviously differ in this context. In all of these cases, you will need to be sensitive to the possibility of conflict of interest. If in doubt, it is better not to ask for a referral than to risk derailing a relationship.

Whether you decide to seek a referral during a phone conversation or in a face-to-face meeting, the conversation needs to be planned like any other. Use the meeting planner we looked at in Chapter 7 to work out your word choice for the aim of the conversation and the results you seek. Rather than questions to identify what drives the client, you will need to consider how to describe the referral you seek, in the terms outlined above: your perfect client, the problem and the benefits you will deliver.

Asking for referrals is simply another part of your routine marketing activity. Like the other marketing elements, it is a matter of planning how to do it most effectively, the frequency of contacts needed to achieve the results you want in terms of additional business and the time that must be allocated. As a guide, I expect to spend around 80 per cent of the time that is not taken up with client delivery on marketing and sales activities. The remainder is divided between business administration (typically only around 5 per cent as I outsource everything I can) and my own CPD.

Many people in the professions find marketing and selling hard; they are not temperamentally suited to it and/or fear possible rejection. That in turn can give rise to a tendency to over-talk during meetings, to tell prospective clients all about themselves rather than asking questions, etc. If the process is planned so that you have a clear and easily articulated reason for making a phone call, many of these issues fall away. However, many people find it helpful to set themselves a target of making a certain number of 'marketing and selling' calls each week or to spend a certain amount of time 'drumming up new business'.

I feel that it is more effective to set a target for a number of calls rather than time spent because it is too easy to allow (or to encourage?) oneself to extend the length of one call to avoid the need to make a second. In order to avoid the 'sine wave revenue' problem, one needs to spend more time on marketing and selling, and in particular on the generation of high quality referrals, than one might wish. That leads us into the topic of strategic account leadership.

Strategic account leadership (SAL)

More commonly called 'strategic account management' or 'SAM', SAL is an approach to help you ensure that those clients who are likely to be the winners of tomorrow both in their own business field and for you are given optimal attention. This has been described as managing politics in three dimensions: within your own firm, within the client firm and externally (ie within the market generally, with your own and the client's suppliers and with the client's customers).

You will need to be able to deliver the total capability of your own firm to address the needs of the client or rather the level of resources appropriate to the needs of the client, when set against the competing needs of other clients. Resources are inevitably constrained and must therefore be allocated appropriately. I think of this as a 'leadership' process rather than 'management' because I feel that part of my role with the clients I select for SAL is to enable them to see opportunities they might not have considered rather than simply to involve myself in their decision-taking processes at the earliest possible moment. In other words, I seek to influence the direction and development of their business.

With one of my clients, I enabled the primary buyer to see the value of an approach that differed markedly from the one he had planned and to make the changes necessary to follow that path successfully. As a result, as he said subsequently, one new division in his firm would produce more in its first year of operation than the rest of the business put together.

A conventional SAM approach would be directed at maximizing my share of that client's business; it would be more for my benefit in maximizing my 'share of wallet'. By contrast, SAL is directed at maximizing the success of the client's business by using my expertise – with the secondary expectation that this will enhance my relationship with that client and the hope that this in turn may lock out possible competitors in my field. The benefit of this type of approach is to ensure that you can take the level of relationship up to that of true partnership as rapidly as possible and maintain it over extended periods of time. That in turn will lock out competitors (including the 'unseen competitors' of 'do nothing' and the use of internal resources). The latter is usually done on grounds of *relative* cost, without a real understanding of the *total* cost and the relative value delivered; it is seen as the cheap option.

SAL looks at two aspects of the client relationship: which clients are of strategic importance to you and your firm, and how to approach the relationship with the primary and other buyers in these accounts in a manner that is strategic rather than tactical. A strategic client relationship is not necessarily defined by the relative level of your fee revenue from that client firm: in other words, current size does matter but only to a degree. More important in my view is the future value of the relationship, ie its potential. You should be looking for the client firms that are likely to be dominant in their field tomorrow not necessarily the blue chips of today.

In that context, one of the most important issues is the position of the firm in its market and whether or to what extent it may be able to outstrip competitors. That may occur as a result of developing or exploiting new technology, growth through acquisition or organically, the formation of a strategic partnership to exploit a new geographic market, etc. What is a relatively small firm today may well become dominant in the future (there are numerous examples, especially in the world of technology and online business). You need, if possible, to become recognized as an enabler of that dominance.

In deciding which clients and prospective clients you wish to treat as strategic accounts, you should once again go back to your definition of a 'perfect client'.

Rather than looking simply at the clients that match closely that definition today, you now need to look forward to imagine the future potential of each client firm. Consider what factors represent current strengths or potential weaknesses for each firm. Look at how you might help each firm to leverage their strengths or minimize the impact of a weakness. Think about the values and behaviours of the senior team and the overall culture of the firm. Are these the kind of people you want to work with and indeed to become allied with?

Having begun to think about client firms/potential client firms that appear to be of possible strategic importance to you in the future, the next step is to carry out a short analysis of where you feel able to add most value most rapidly for each firm. In other words, you are looking for the future commercial fit. That fit may not exist immediately but the key is what could be possible given your involvement and how best to articulate that to the relevant primary buyer. Of course your own business will not remain static; it too will develop in terms of reach, available resources and capability. These developments will need to be added into the mix.

As well as the future potential for a given client firm, you will need to factor in the cost to you of delivering your value to that firm. Work that requires regular, long-distance travel may appear superficially attractive but the profitability may in fact be low once you take into account the time and cash cost of the necessary travel.

Within any client firm (and certainly within any large client firm) there are likely to be many different functions and business units. It is unlikely that you will be dealing with all of them simultaneously. For the purposes of SAL, therefore, your client/potential client will be only the part of the overall firm with which you will be working. In the interest of focus, it is helpful to narrow your definition of 'the client' as much as practicable. For example, you may work with a major global bank, 'ABC Bank plc'. For this purpose it is not the bank that is the client, but for example the London HQ, or rather the IT department of the London HQ. Better yet it could be the XYZ project team within the IT department of the London HQ of ABC Bank.

The reason for this drilling down is not only focusing your efforts and reducing what amounts to a corporate elephant to some of its component, bite-sized chunks, but also to recognize that the needs and drivers of the micro-client will not be the same as those of the macro-client. Failure to recognize this and act accordingly is likely to lead you to focus on the wrong commercial fit opportunity for the primary buyer to whom you have access. This approach also helps you to match the way you market and sell your services to the way in which the client buys in terms of geographic and functional responsibilities and budget allocations. In other words, it helps you to focus on a different set of buyer roles that will be better aligned to your delivery capability; you will sell the optimal value to the right people.

TABLE 9.1   How the client sees you

Level	Description
5	An External Business Partner (EBP). Recognized as a critical enabler of strategic delivery. A key team member but not actually on the payroll. Adds expertise, etc not available in house. Feels like 'one of us'. Our 'go-to' person.
4	Contributes to the bottom line either by enabling revenue enhancement or cost reduction and goes out of their way to find ways to add value for us.
3	Provides good service and business support.
2	Offers a product/service that is objectively above average. A safe pair of hands.
1	Meets the standard specification and offers competitive prices

Having identified the best micro-clients that you feel able to treat strategically, you now need to assess where your relationship sits with each of them. This is a variation on the relationship pyramid that we looked at in Chapter 7. It focuses not on the level of personal relationship but on the way that the client perceives you and the value you are able to deliver. I think of this in terms of five levels, shown in Table 9.1.

You will gain an objective view of how the client sees you and your firm by asking the client directly, if you can (if you don't feel able to do so, the relationship is probably less good than you hoped). You can also think about the nature of your conversations with the client and at what level in the client firm you are working and having those conversations. The higher the level in the client hierarchy at which you engage routinely and the more 'personal' the conversation (whether at a personal level or in terms of business criticality/confidentiality) the higher up the scale your relationship.

It is also helpful to look at the changes that you know have taken place over the previous 12–18 months within the client firm and what changes you expect to see over the same period in the future. The former will indicate the degree to which (for example) the firm may be overwhelmed by the volume or pace of change internally and hence be unwilling to undertake a project which, although beneficial, may need yet more change/reorganization to execute. The latter may indicate opportunities for a commercial fit and/or cultural change that could align the firm more closely with the values and behaviours that help to define a 'perfect client' for you.

The next step is to consider how the client firm (or your chosen element of it) sees the world: their market, their position relative to competitors, the trends and opportunities for them and for their industry, how they measure success, etc. You should also seek to understand how the client views people like you and your firm. Do they have a history of working with your firm? How was that for them (and for you)? With whom and at what level do you have contact? How long ago was the most recent contact? Does it seem likely that the client believes that you understand them and their business? More important, to what extent do they believe that you understand their clients and the needs of those clients?

So far as possible you should assess your own competitors in the same manner. Don't forget to include in that assessment in-house resources – the potential for a DIY approach rather than hiring you. The matrix in Table 9.2 will help you to capture and evaluate the relevant data in a reasonably objective manner.

As a final step in evaluating possible candidates for a SAL approach, you should consider the degree to which you can align individuals within your own firm with the relevant counterpart within the client firm. This is of course in the context of a given commercial opportunity that you have identified and which is relevant to the micro-client on which you are focusing. For example, let us say that your micro-client is a project team within the London IT department of a global bank, which is charged with the delivery of an online credit risk assessment tool for small businesses. Almost regardless of the role you seek with the client, you will ideally be able to field a team from your firm that can engage as equals with:

- the head of small business lending for the bank;
- the head of the bank's London IT function;
- the business analyst who set the deliverables for the project;
- the project coordinator or manager;
- individual work stream leaders (and perhaps those actually involved in coding).

By 'engage as equals' I mean not necessarily that they are at an equivalent level in the corporate hierarchy but that they speak the same kind of language. A work stream leader in an IT project is likely to prefer to talk to a fellow IT technician/programmer than to someone who has no direct experience in this field. It will allow them to communicate more easily because both have common if not shared experiences and language/terms of art. If you are a solo-preneur, this may be hard to achieve unless you focus your definition of the micro-client sufficiently.

These considerations need not take long; indeed most of them can be undertaken without the need for formal analysis as such. The aim is to identify client firms that are of the greatest potential importance for you in the future.

TABLE 9.2 Client firm's relative positioning

Focus area	Factors to consider	Score 1–10 (where 10 is most positive)
World view	Economic growth trends	
	Political risks likely to affect the client's business	
	Currency trends	
Market/ industry view	Maturity of the client's industry (eg new industry = higher risk but more potential opportunity for innovation)	
	Known/likely innovations in this industry and the client's position relative to these (ie are they likely to be left behind by new innovations?)	
	Public perceptions of industry growth prospects	
Client firm's relative position in its own market	Ranking of firm in its industry group (NB bigger may not always be better; eg a smaller firm may be more innovative/nimble)	
	Number of direct competitors	
	Profitability relative to competitors	
Strengths, threats and opportunities	Positioning relative to new technology	
	Potential for merger or acquisition (or is the client likely to be a target)?	
	Clearly defined USP for client firm	
	Clear strength or weakness that offers your firm a commercial fit	

TABLE 9.2   *continued*

Focus area	Factors to consider	Score 1–10 (where 10 is most positive)
Success measures	Do you know how the client measures their own success and yours?	
	To what extent are their values/success measures congruent with yours?	
History	Have you worked successfully with the client previously?	
	Has the client worked successfully with your competitors?	
	How positive was the experience for the client in working with you/your competitors?	
	Client believes you understand them and have their interests at heart	
	Client believes you understand their customers and the value they offer them	
	Total (maximum 200):	

Once you have an idea of the relevant macro- and micro-clients, you can decide quite easily what your strategic aim is for each of them. In other words, you can decide where you would like to get to with each client and over what timeframe. You should be able to write this down in the form of a strategic aim statement, which should cover:

- your definition of the micro-client;
- the commercial fit;
- the value you expect to deliver;
- the benefits/results that the client will experience;
- the benefit to you (which may not be in pure profit terms).

You will now be in a position to plan at least the initial steps to achieve these strategic aims. Each of those steps must lead towards the strategic aim. That strategic aim will remain constant, but the planned interim steps will almost certainly change over time. It is important to break down each step to as granular a level as is reasonable so that each builds on the last and serves to create a solid foundation for the next. Each should be forward-looking rather than developed from what has already occurred in the past.

It is helpful to be able to articulate your strategic aim from the standpoint of the micro-client and in terms that relate to the relationship and the role you seek with that client. As an example, consider something like:

> Our strategic aim in working with ABC Bank is to be seen as the most important external partner in marketing strategy by the Small Business Risk Project team of their London IT division and as the people who enabled them to gain insight into the benefits sought by small business customers using the online assessment system so that they could avoid undue complexity, thus saving time and development cost in producing the most user-friendly system of its type in the UK.

So far as possible, develop these ideas as a team within your own firm and test them with the client. What seems obvious to you may be less so to your colleagues and to the client. This will help to ensure that what you seek to deliver by way of value is aligned with how the micro-client sees its own mission and needs. It helps them to focus on the specific opportunity that you have identified and where you are now, in effect, co-designing a solution. You can ensure that what is proposed does in fact play to your strengths and also help the client to overcome a weakness.

A further useful reality check is the extent to which the strategic aim is achievable within the desired timeframe and the degree to which its achievement is expected to enhance your personal and professional relationship with the client. Which of the buyers within the client firm will benefit and how? Are those benefits relevant in that they touch some of the 'hot buttons' that drive the client's emotional decision making? Is the language that you will use to articulate these benefits such that it is likely to resonate with the client, based on your understanding of their emotional drivers and learning preference? (Think back to your initial meeting as outlined in Chapter 7.)

How to use SAL in practice

Not all clients can be strategic accounts nor can you act strategically with all clients; in some cases it is not something that will be required or appreciated and if you attempt to treat them as strategic accounts they may perceive themselves to be over-serviced and hence over-charged. (I have in mind a restaurant to which I was taken by a client where at least eight different waiters brought different parts of the meal or carried out jobs such as pouring water or sweeping crumbs off the table. The food was mediocre and the bill enormous. It was not a good experience.)

The steps in an effective use of SAL are in outline as follows:

- Assess the client firms that appear to be of strategic importance to you in the future.
- Define why that may be in terms of opportunities that you can help the client to leverage or weaknesses you can help to overcome.
- Check that the client sees similar opportunities. Leadership is involved in helping clients to envisage and grasp opportunities that they have not yet seen for themselves – even though this is likely to require a longer and more difficult sales process.
- Conserve your own resources by selecting only those clients where you believe a SAL approach will enable you to win more business that is more profitable and also to enhance your relationship level and the level of value which the client perceives you bring to them (see Table 9.1).
- Define the micro-client and your strategic aim: confirm with the client. This is of course also a key part of your tactical sales process as well as a necessary element of SAL. The strategic aim will be based on the drivers you identify with the client during your initial meeting and other early 'pre-project' meetings.
- Align your team with the relevant individuals within the micro-client and ensure that the necessary communication channels are opened and maintained and that relevant information is captured and shared across your whole team. Where possible, treat the client as part of your team and involve them in the communication process.
- Ensure that you have the necessary resources for delivery and for maintenance of the relationships and that you yourself are able to manage both closely and to control the use of resources (some of which may be in demand from other parallel projects).
- Gain agreement to proceed with the initial engagement; manage delivery closely and attempt to exceed expectations. Check that the returns you expected in terms of profit and enhanced relationship are in fact achieved. If not, examine why and what could be done to improve the position.
- Communicate constantly both internally and with the client on current delivery and future opportunities.
- Review your list of strategic accounts constantly and be willing to downgrade any that no longer fit your selection criteria. This is vital to conserve your limited resources (and they are always limited) even though it may force you to operate outside your comfort zone in developing new client relationships or extending current ones.

This leads naturally to the penultimate chapter where we look at the systems and processes in your business that will allow you to ensure consistency of delivery and a positive experience for clients, and to eliminate the 'feast or famine' situation in revenue terms. This approach will help to secure repeat business and referrals and indirectly to enhance profitability because fee rates cease to be a major issue in negotiations with clients and prospects. It will help you to focus with confidence on those clients you can realistically consider as being of strategic importance to you and with whom you most enjoy working and can deliver greatest value.

Building systems into your business

10

In this chapter we look at systems. This is not simply IT systems (although there may be a need for IT as an enabler of your systems). It is far more to do with the type of systems thinking and the business processes that help to ensure that nothing is left to chance and that your clients receive the same consistently high level of service throughout their relationship with you and your firm. If yours is a larger firm (more than a handful of staff) those same systems can allow you to hand over a project to a colleague without fear of a hiatus in the event of an emergency. If you are a solo-preneur, they will help you to ensure that you (literally) get it all done and do not have a residual fear that something vital has been forgotten.

As you build your portfolio of work, you will begin to develop a body of knowledge that can become valuable in its own right, not least because it can help you to avoid reinventing the wheel. That can occur only to the extent that you have a system for capturing, accessing and applying your corporate knowledge. We have previously touched on CRM systems that help you to stay in touch with clients in a structured manner and to track your firm's relationships across multiple clients, functions and geographies. CRM is important but it is by no means the only element of your business that will benefit from a systems approach.

Good systems will help you to focus with confidence on those clients that you can realistically consider to be of strategic importance to you, with whom you most enjoy working and to whom you can deliver greatest value. As a result they will tend to be the clients who are most profitable to you partly because they understand the value you deliver and hence price is minimized as an issue in their buying decisions. The key benefit of systems is, however, to save time, which is of course your most important asset, by minimizing errors and re-work and allowing you to focus your efforts.

In this chapter we look at systems thinking in your business from the following perspectives:

- business organization;
- checklists;
- time allocation;
- client relationships and contacts;
- corporate knowledge; and
- documents.

These are linked in many ways and you will gain most benefit only when you act on each of these aspects for your business and, so far as practicable, take advantage of the linkages.

Business organization

Most established businesses have developed organically over a period of time. That is true just as much of a firm comprising one person as it is of a large professional services firm with dozens of staff. That development will tend to be haphazard and to lack structure and there may be a tendency to add people to the payroll, initially on a temporary basis perhaps, who quickly become permanent members of the team. As the firm grows, there may be a felt need to divide into separate departments or functions. Within a short space of time, the firm is unrecognizable and the culture may well begin to change – not always for the better.

This is a common challenge of any growing business: how to manage the growth so that the firm remains lean and profitable with success based on delighting clients. There is also an issue of how to ensure that the creation of personal fiefdoms is minimized. The creation of fiefdoms is sometimes confused with the creation of elites. I see the two issues as inherently different in that a fiefdom tends to be run for the benefit of its metaphorical feudal overlord rather than for the firm as a whole or, more important, for the benefit of its clients. It is an inward-looking mind-set founded on a fear of famine; that business may turn bad and revenue fall; however, if we can protect this fiefdom, we can look after ourselves.

By contrast, the development of an elite within an organization is more commonly the creation of a group to which others aspire; a winning team. It is not unlike military Special Forces; not everyone has the ability to join but anyone that does and who shares the culture of the group is welcomed. Those who complete their tour of duty and go back to their own units take with them the attitudes developed in the Special Forces context which are then trickled down to others. The tendency is to raise the game for the whole of the military rather than locking up expertise and ability in a small group. It is a mind-set of plenty, of sharing and of seeking opportunity.

To ensure that your organizational structure remains fit for purpose, I highly recommend that, as part of your periodic (usually annual) business planning process you ask the question: 'If we were designing this business from scratch, today, to serve the clients we have and those we expect to have in the next 12–18 months, what would it look like?' You should start with a completely blank sheet and try to forget the personalities currently involved – including your own. Think instead of the roles that would need to be filled and the traits and characteristics that would represent a 'perfect' candidate for each role. Next, add the relevant skills sets. Lastly, do a swift 'finger in the air' assessment of your current team against each of the relevant criteria in each role. Where you have individuals in post that would rate 7 or less out of 10 on any given attribute, think about how they can be developed to achieve a rating of 8 or better. If you believe that they cannot be developed to that extent, you may need to review their role in the business. It does not necessarily mean that an individual has no role; only that they may be better deployed elsewhere.

Think about your business from the standpoint of the client, in particular those clients that you would deem to be of strategic importance. How do they see the business today? How would you like them to see it? Where are the gaps? How can they be addressed? Don't allow yourself to be trapped into following structures and patterns of thinking that have worked well (or even just adequately) until now. The value of this exercise is in allowing yourself to consider different approaches and not to reject out of hand something that seems unduly radical. Designing a better organization to serve clients is not the same as implementing that design. The latter will almost certainly throw up many practical problems that either make it impractical to move to the new structure or may only allow it to occur over time.

Don't forget that structural change always imposes pressure on an organization. For people to feel that they are in a constant state of flux and that they lack stability is usually a cause of stress and low morale. Change is easier if it is incremental rather than radical, although there may be a need from time to time for root and branch reorganization. That must be done in the context of a strategic change that will need to be well articulated in advance and clearly bought into (not simply 'understood') by the vast majority of staff at all levels if it is to be successful.

Why do people buy into proposed changes? Because they understand the reason for the change and the benefit to themselves of making it real. It is a case of internal selling. Before embarking on any major organizational change, no matter how 'obvious' it may appear to you that it is necessary, make sure that you can answer positively each of the questions in the checklist in Table 10.1.

TABLE 10.1 Questions to consider before reorganizing

Key issue	Drilling down
What are the benefits to your clients and to your people of the change you seek to make? What is the downside?	• How will you explain this to clients and to your own direct reports? • What will make them buy in and not just say 'Yes'? • What will make it easy for them to sell it to their colleagues? • Can you pilot test it before you go ahead?
Is the change worth the inevitable disruption and cost?	• How will you both *judge* and *take* the benefits of the change? • Are the projected benefits achievable? • Are the timeframe and budget realistic? • How will you quantify the degree of disruption?
Is the organization ready for a change to its structure? Who wants it and why?	• Could a structural change actually harm the organization and its ability to serve clients? • Are senior individuals within the firm demanding this type of change? • If the changes do not occur, how will this affect clients and staff?
Why do you want this change?	• What are the benefits to clients? How will you tell them? • Will it make your job easier (even if it makes the jobs of others harder)? • Could it give rise to unintended consequences?
Do you have enough power to make the change happen (ie to overcome resistance)?	• Do you have enough internal support and resources? • Do you have enough powerful allies? • Will they stick with you? • Who will oppose you and why?
Are your people already overwhelmed by change?	• Are your people and/or clients 'changed out'? • Are there currently 'too many moving pieces'?
Could you pull the plug?	• How will you know it is time to stop? • Who will take the decision to pull the plug? • Would this be seen by your people and/or by clients as a personal failure by you?
Did you ask the right questions of the right people to ensure that this change would be welcomed by clients?	• Who is asking for the change and why? • What 'drives' them? • Who benefits? Do they buy in? • Who might suffer? How to mitigate that? • What is the potential downside?

Before making a proposal for organizational change, I recommend that you draft the letter that you will send to clients explaining the reasons for the change and the benefits to them. I suggest that you then prepare a PowerPoint® deck (or an internal e-mail) doing the same thing for your colleagues. If either is hard to write or if you find it hard to talk through the PowerPoint® deck in a way that you find convincing, it is probably wise to reconsider. Try the letter and the deck on trusted colleagues – ie those who you trust to act as honest devil's advocates – and assess their reaction.

A former boss of mine would apply what she called the '*Private Eye* test' to any significant business change or opportunity. The test was simple: would we as a leadership team be embarrassed if what we were considering were to be reported in the satirical magazine *Private Eye*? How likely was it that it would be featured there? A sound guiding principle in considering changes is the degree to which they benefit clients. If there is little or no benefit, it is almost certainly not worth making the change.

When considering organization structure it is also necessary to think about governance. That is not simply who reports to whom; what the hierarchy looks like. It is more to do with ensuring that information flows around the firm and to/from clients as readily as possible and that it is not only accessible to those that need it but is also readily available. In reviewing your firm's structure a key component is internal communication flows and mechanisms:

- What information must be communicated?
- By whom?
- To whom?
- By when/how often?
- By what means?
- What will they do as a result?

As a default, most firms set up communication mechanisms that are far too complex and seek to pass far too much information to be effective. Few people can hold more than seven or eight facts in their mind at any given time. It is unlikely therefore that decisions will be taken effectively if the number of factors on which they must be based exceeds that number.

Checklists

It is often said that long practice can engender a state of unconscious competence, rather in the manner of learning to drive a car. When we first sit behind a steering wheel we are only too well aware (conscious) of our own incompetence as a driver. Over time we eventually become competent but remain conscious of what we are doing every moment we are behind the wheel. A little time after passing the driving test, we begin to lose the felt need for conscious awareness or focus on every aspect of what we are doing as we drive. That may lead to the occasional 'near miss' or perhaps to a collision, which quickly reasserts consciousness of what we are doing. Eventually we attain 'unconscious competence' which allows us to drive almost on auto-pilot with the actions required to drive safely being undertaken at a sub-conscious level. We may drive several miles with no recollection of the journey.

In the world of professional services (and indeed in many other fields) that type of unconscious activity can lead to errors through omission: we simply forget to do something that is routine, because it is just that – routine. A solution to that forgetfulness which has been deployed successfully in the medical field, in the military and in the airline industry is the humble checklist.

Perhaps the best description I have seen of how to develop and use check-lists effectively is in the book *The Checklist Manifesto* by Atul Gawande, an American surgeon who pioneered their use in hospitals in the United States. The use of checklists by junior nurses to monitor the actions of senior doctors in routine matters such as swabbing the arm of a patient before taking blood or administering an injection served massively to reduce hospital-acquired infections, saved lives and consequently saved large amounts of money for the hospitals themselves.

In a professional services business, checklists can serve to ensure that nothing is forgotten at any key stage of a project. In preparing a letter of confirmation for a new piece of work, for example, it would be a simple matter to list the key elements that must be included in such a document. For example:

- Results required by the client.
- Success factors for this project.
- Potential blocking factors.
- Key stakeholders.
- Outline approach/process.
- Resources to be provided by the client.
- Resources to be provided by your firm.
- Resources provided by others.
- Who is to lead the project and coordinate resourcing.
- Governance.
- Fees and terms of payment.
- Start and end dates of the project, etc.

It may seem onerous to create checklists for each aspect of your business, especially if yours is a small firm or especially if you are a solo-preneur. The benefits are significant, however, in that the chance of errors is much reduced. The result is to save time and to minimize potential embarrassment with a client. Having and using checklists also obviates the need to remember what needs to be done, which enhances your focus on activities that truly add value and reduces distraction. The development and use of checklists also helps to 'on-board' new staff more quickly and can help in the development of a systems manual for your business which, a) facilitates its rapid growth and, b) can make it more saleable if and when you seek an exit, because it is replicable rather than reliant on what's in your head.

When you decide to use checklists in your business, it is important that everyone does in fact use them and that any member of staff, no matter how junior, has the absolute right to call a halt to an activity if a step is missed. If there is an ego issue about this it will be hard to gain the full benefit of using a checklist.

Time allocation

Time is your most important asset. It cannot be managed, only allocated: once a unit of time has been used, it cannot be recycled as such. It is of course possible to do a piece of work once and be paid for it many times (for example developing an online training programme where the delivery is automated following an automated sign-up and payment process). That option is relatively rare in a professional services context and indeed it is for this reason that many professionals seek to charge for their time rather than for results delivered (input versus output).

Time allocation is about effectiveness versus efficiency. Efficiency in this context means doing things more rapidly and where possible doing more things concurrently. Effectiveness is about doing more of the *right* things to a level that is fit for purpose rather than (necessarily) to a standard of perfection. The incremental effort and time needed to take a piece of work from an effective 90 per cent solution delivered in a timely manner to a 100 per cent solution (that may be delivered late) is typically in my experience at least half as much again and anything up to double the input needed to achieve the effective, timely 90 per cent.

So as to allocate time effectively it is necessary to decide what the 'right things' are for you and for your business. This means capturing and prioritizing all of the tasks you have on your 'to do' list, whether personal or professional. In the interests of simplicity, I use a basic three-tier approach to prioritization:

- **A** = tasks where the results contribute directly to the success of the business either by way of revenue generation or because they are a regulatory requirement. These tasks will typically have a deadline. I would include in this category tax and regulatory returns for the business and personal tasks such as filing my own tax return or buying a birthday gift for my child, as well as any marketing or sales activity that is intended to lead directly to revenue within the next 90 days or less.

- **B** = tasks that are not necessarily direct contributors to the success of the business or do not have a deadline that is close to hand. That could include preparing a piece of marketing collateral that will not necessarily lead to revenue directly, or indeed completing my personal tax return to the extent that it is not due to be filed for at least 30 days.

- **C** = tasks that I would like to do. They have no deadline and do not contribute meaningfully to the success of the business. That might include clearing out old research material or Photoshopping some of my digital photographs.

Having allocated a simple priority to each task on my list, I can then assess how long each of the A and B tasks is likely to take. The standard of completion is an effective 90 per cent that is fit for purpose. Tasks will expand to take up the time available, so the time assessment needs to be realistic but not unduly generous.

The next step is to allocate your available time, having decided on the length of your working day. This may seem to be a strange concept to those who have worked in a professional services environment for any length of time. Surely the day extends until either the work is done or we fall asleep at the desk? I have certainly experienced that kind of approach and indeed worked in organizations where it was a norm and long hours were a badge of honour. Research indicates, however, that people do not work effectively for more than about 10 hours each day for extended periods. Of course you can work longer on occasion. To do so routinely will usually lead to a degradation of performance. It tends to create stress and I am reliably informed by a friend who is trained as a psychologist that 'stress makes you stupid'; apparently this is clinically proven.

Your time allocation needs to cater not only for your work tasks but also for your own needs such as adequate sleep (how long you will sleep without an alarm – typically 7.5 hours or more), physical exercise and eating proper meals at least twice a day, one of which should be breakfast. The benefit is that if you allow time to do these things and indeed *take* the time to do them, you will feel better, your performance will improve and in most cases your colleagues and clients will find you easier to work with.

Break your working day into 15 minute slots. Starting with your 'A' tasks plan backwards from the deadline in each case, allocating enough time to complete the task by the time it is due and ideally beforehand. It is usually easier to break a large task into smaller chunks. For example, it may take me three hours to write an article for a professional journal. I generally find it better to change focus after the first couple of hours and go back to edit and polish what I have written. I would therefore allocate one block of 2 hours and one block of 1 hour to complete the article. The second block will be at least the day before the article is due to be received. Once I have used up the allotted time, the article must be complete or else I must reallocate time from another task (hence the importance of being realistic with your time estimates).

During any given working day, at least 70 per cent of the time available must be allocated to 'A' tasks. It may need to be 100 per cent on some days. To the extent that there is time available, I can allocate up to 20 per cent to 'B' tasks. If there is still time left over, I can allocate up to 10 per cent of the day to 'C' tasks. The reality is that 'C' tasks rarely, if ever, get done unless you choose to upgrade them to at least 'B' status. However, by allocating time in this manner you can give yourself permission to drop those tasks that are, objectively, unimportant. The benefit is that they do not clutter your mental 'in tray' and cause distraction.

One of your 'A' tasks for each day must be a 'meeting with me', which should be at least 15 minutes in length and allows you to plan the coming day or two, review your priorities and simply prepare yourself. I find that it is better for me to do this at the start of the day; others find it is better to use the last 15–30 minutes of the day instead. It matters little so long as you take the time. The benefit is to gain a greater sense of control over your environment and to feel that you know what you need to do. It is also a way to adjust priorities in a controlled manner rather than allowing yourself to be buffeted by events.

Another 'A' task is to allocate time to deal with the normal flow of e-mails and other communications that arrive during a typical day. I try to limit the use of e-mail to three blocks of time during the day: early on following or immediately before my 'meeting with me', just before lunch time, and late afternoon. In addition, I use what would otherwise be 'dead' time such as travel between client meetings to handle routine e-mails, phone calls, etc using my BlackBerry®.

In handling routine communications I adopt what I call the '4D' approach:

1 Do it – so long as it will take less than 5 minutes (for example respond to a meeting request).

2 Defer it – but allocate a specific priority and time to the task and defer only once.

3 Delegate it – but only so long as the person to whom you delegate has the ability and the authority to do the job as you would do it.

4 Drop it – but tell others who may be involved that you are doing so.

Delegation is something of an art. It is often used, especially in larger firms, to pass responsibility but not necessarily control. If delegation is to be effective, it is essential that the person to whom you delegate has:

● adequate knowledge and experience to do the job;

● clear authority to do the job (in other words they are recognized and accepted by others involved or affected as 'speaking with your voice') and budget where required;

- well-defined parameters or 'span of decision' within which to operate and that provide a framework within which the individual can change the approach to delivery or even change the desired end result if need be;

- a clear understanding of how success is to be judged including the timeframe for delivery.

If any of these is lacking it is likely that the delegated task will end up back on your desk but with added complexity or problems. It is also neither fair to try to delegate something that is essentially 'broken' nor is it likely to result in success. This is a variation on the theme 'You can't outsource cr*p.'

Client relationships and contacts

We have already looked at CRM in Chapter 8. There is no need to repeat the information on systems, etc contained there. That said, it is hard to over-estimate the importance of an effective system to manage client relationships and contacts. The benefit is that it takes away the need for you to remember to do what is required to maintain contact appropriately with multiple clients and prospective clients.

In a very small business it need be no more than the electronic equivalent of a set of index cards on which you record the contact details for each client and prospective client plus a note of the actual contacts made. In the days before computers were widely used in business, I was sales director for a major mutual funds company. I used a Filofax to keep client records, simply because I could pick it up and carry it with me. Most of my colleagues used three sets of index cards: one for active clients, one for clients that were inactive (or had done no business for six months or more) and one for prospective clients. It would be unusual not to use some form of spreadsheet or database for the same purpose now that technology is used so universally, but it could be done.

Most businesses will benefit from the use of some form of dedicated contact management system. However, the system is of value only to the extent that the data is current and accurate. If the use of the system is simply a by-product of your normal routine it is far more likely that it will remain current and hence be used and useful. For example, to use something like Sage's ACT® not only as a database but as the way you send e-mails, dial a client's phone number, etc will automatically ensure that the client contact records are up to date. What is hard to automate is your resolve to design and use a system to follow-up with clients and contacts.

Like the development and use of checklists, there is an element of time investment needed to design and implement a client contact system. The benefits of doing so, in terms of the development of your business and clients' perceptions of your interest in them as individuals, more than justify that investment. Indeed the more effort you put in at the outset, the greater the likely return on that investment of effort and the more rapidly you will see it.

Corporate knowledge and documents

I am combining an overview of these two aspects of business systems because there is a considerable degree of overlap between them in terms of the way they work and the content.

In a law firm, what I have termed 'corporate knowledge' might be thought of as 'precedents'. It is the combined recollection of what you and your colleagues have done for clients in the past plus your collective learning gained as a result of academic study and experience. Much of that knowledge will be contained in documents of one sort or another, be it letters to clients, PowerPoint® decks, spreadsheets, e-mail traffic, etc. Much of it will simply reside in the heads of individuals and will exit the business when they do unless efforts are made to capture and store the knowledge in a way that is accessible to others and easily searchable. The issue is how to access the information contained in those documents so that you can use it in ways that help you to avoid reinvention.

At its simplest conceptual level, you can think of your documents/knowledge base as a filing system. For a very small business, you might need only one file for each client plus, perhaps, a 'topic' file that contains notes of where in those clients files reference is made to a given topic or even perhaps a summary. In a somewhat larger firm, you might choose to have files held for each function within your business or for each location, for example, and then break down information by client below that. At the simple 'one client, one file' level, it is not necessarily a major issue whether you hold documents in hard copy or in electronic form. The problems begin to arise when you need to see a complete picture of a given client, for example, that spans multiple functions, geographies, etc.

In this type of situation one needs either a well-designed electronic system or a well-thought out filing system with highly intelligent and knowledgeable human oversight. In my experience the latter is now uncommon but in some cases has proved to be more effective and arguably cheaper to implement. For example, the staff at some of the major academic libraries such as the Bodleian in Oxford or the British Library in London have an almost encyclopaedic knowledge of material available on given topics. It is a mistake to dismiss the importance of human intelligence in making connections between diverse pieces of data. It is the system design that allows a human 'stranger' to know that the data exists.

Even for relatively small businesses, it is hard to see how knowledge and documents can be held and used effectively other than by way of an electronic system that holds the material in a form that is searchable. At a basic level, one can achieve a lot with files held in pdf format that allows text to be searched. That sort of functionality can be achieved reasonably cheaply using Adobe's Acrobat® Pro.

In order to implement any data/knowledge management system success-fully the starting point is not how you want to file documents but how you want to access them and search within them. As my PA informed me some-what tartly many years ago, the purpose of a filing system is to be able to locate information easily, not to get it out of sight for ever, like the Ark in the final scene of the film *Raiders of the Lost Ark*.

Full-scale document management systems can be costly and are usually hard to implement well. There is a tendency to make them unduly complex and prescriptive in terms of the way in which they are used and maintained and how information can be searched. Replicating the manner in which search engines such as Google® use key-word-based searches to locate documents or other information opens massive opportunities.

A detailed examination of knowledge and information management is beyond the scope of this book. However, it is vital to consider how to address the issue in your own business. Key success factors include:

- Keep the system structure as simple as you can.
- Time spent in refining the design of a system before implementing it invariably pays dividends.
- Minimize the need so far as possible for manual indexing.
- Make knowledge/document management a by-product of the normal business process of producing the material in the first instance rather than adding a separate 'library' process.
- Ensure that searching your data is simple and produces comprehensive results in a user-friendly manner.
- Recognize that there is a learning curve in building and using any such system but that perseverance yields huge benefits over time.
- Make sure that everyone uses the system and keeps it up to date. Knowledge is of no use to the business if it is locked in the head of an individual. There may need to be a carrot and stick approach to ensuring that knowledge is shared rather that retained, whether intentionally or by accident. In other words, make this part of routine appraisal for each staff member.

Data backup

There is a saying in the US Marine Corps that 'One is none.' In other words, if you do not have a backup, you may find yourself with nothing. That is especially true of data that is held in electronic form, although the principle extends to hard copy material also. In the UK, it is a legal requirement to keep client data secure, with heavy fines as a sanction if one is found not to have done so.

Backup need not be difficult but it is essential. One of the main reasons is that the hard disk drives which form the data storage medium for the vast majority of computers (the exception is those relatively few machines that use solid state or 'Flash' drives) are inherently prone to mechanical failure. This is because the data is stored on a magnetic disk that spins at high speed – typically 5,400 or 7,200 revolutions per minute. They simply wear out over time. Over the last 10 years I have experienced three hard disk failures in my personal laptop (which I understand is about average for a heavily-used machine) and one motherboard failure (which is far less common). Without good backup the loss of data would have been catastrophic for my business on any one of those occasions.

Basic backup for a single machine can be achieved by copying data to a separate external hard drive connected by a USB cable. That external drive can then be disconnected and stored in a separate, secure location: separate in case of, for example, fire or theft. There are pieces of software that can be used to create a mirror image of what is on the hard drive on your machine – including the program files as well as your own data. I have used Acronis True Image for this purpose on my personal laptop with a weekly backup routine in two locations: home and office. I still carry out the home backup over the weekend and the office one mid-week so that there is no more than a three-day gap between backups. If one is lost, the other will be not more than one week out of date. There are many other pieces of software that fulfil the same function as Acronis.

This process of course requires manual effort and that I remember to do the job. There are three options that can automate the process and make it more robust: online backup (a 'cloud-based solution'), a Network Attached Storage device or NAS drive; or the use of a server. I have used two online backup systems: the US-based Carbonite and Squirrelsave provided by the UK-based firm, Memset. Both work in a similar manner. Having paid for the service of your choice, you download a piece of software onto your computer. Thereafter, whenever the machine is connected to the internet, the backup service accesses the machine to see what files have been added or changed. These are encrypted and copied onto a server located at the provider's premises. In the event that you need to recover data, you access your account using a pre-set password and recover either a single file or the entire contents of your hard disk in the event of a catastrophic loss of data. The service is automated and secure to the extent that it is encrypted.

There are two potential downsides. First, the transfer of data is slow and the speed is limited by the volume of data in relation to the speed of your internet connection. I have never had to recover data from either service but to recover a complete hard drive would be a daunting task that could take several days. Second, if you use a US-based service, your data is subject to the provisions of the Patriot Act which (in outline) means that it can be accessed at will by US law enforcement agencies. In some cases, such as UK government data, there is a regulatory requirement that it may not be stored on servers outside the EU.

Nonetheless, an automated online backup is an excellent safety factor, especially for a solo-preneur or small business. I feel that this type of online solution is a good choice as a 'belt and braces' or 'backup backup' in addition to something like Acronis and the manual system outlined above.

A NAS drive is essentially a dedicated 'box' that does nothing but store data and allow it to be shared across a network. It can also be accessed remotely and securely from any machine that has internet access. A NAS drive can have multiple hard disks (usually two or four bays are available but there can be more). The benefit is that the disks can be set up in what is known as a RAID format (Redundant Array of Independent Disks). That allows a variety of approaches to duplication of data within the machine. For practical purposes, mirroring is in my view the best approach. That means that, if the NAS has two drives, each will be a mirror image of the other. Therefore, if one drive fails, you still have complete backup and the opportunity simply to replace the failed drive. A perfectly sound basic NAS drive can be bought for around £200. The cost of hard disks to slot into the NAS drive bays will vary depending on their storage capacity, but a 1 Terabyte (1,000 Gigabytes) drive can be bought currently for less than £80: storage capacity is amazingly cheap.

A server is a more robust version of a NAS but offers essentially similar functionality in terms of backup. Cost of a basic server can be in the low hundreds of pounds depending on how much storage capacity you elect to use and how many separate drives. It will also offer much more by way of data management and sharing facilities and indeed one can use a server for hosting websites, running your own e-mail system, etc. The server can be located at your own premises or you can rent a dedicated or virtual private server from any of the web hosting companies that abound. The monthly rent for a virtual private server can be less than £50. However, there are usually multiple 'optional extras' that will increase the cost considerably. While I would have no compunction in setting up and managing a NAS drive at my office or home, I would not wish to go through the learning curve of setting up and managing a server. Unless you have the necessary skills set or have a staff member who does, I would opt for the hosted approach.

Why bother with systems?

Putting in place systems within your business may seem onerous. Some investment of time and effort is indeed needed. However, once the necessary systems are in place, the business can begin to run almost on auto-pilot because the vast majority of routine 'stuff' is handled either automatically or can be dealt with using minimal effort. The benefit is that you and more of your colleagues can focus on the critical functions of revenue generation, client relationship management, strategic account leadership and delivery of work of the highest quality.

These same systems will allow you to 'on-board' new staff more rapidly, reduce error rates and re-work and minimize distractions. A systematized business is usually a more saleable business. There is a time cost in designing and implementing systems that are relevant and useful for your particular business, but it is time very well spent.

And so to our final chapter, where we look at the nuts and bolts of bringing it all together: how to implement the ideas contained in this book for your business.

Putting it all together: a one-month implementation plan

11

This final chapter brings together the key ideas from previous chapters in the form of an action plan that will enable you to put in place a full business development programme for your business. The aim is to create multiple streams of concurrent activity rather than doing things sequentially. It also allows you to see the complete picture in what amounts to a 'paint by numbers' form rather than as a set of disconnected activities. While there is some benefit in working in isolation, individually on any of the topics outlined so far, the greatest value is in addressing the issue of business development at a holistic level. We also look at some basics of recruitment; how, in the words of Jim Collins, to 'get the right people on your bus' – one of the most important attributes of the 'great' companies in his much-quoted book *Good to Great.*

Throughout this book I have emphasized the need to plan and prepare. The benefit of planning is to minimize the impact of chance on your business. Market conditions, the vagaries of the economy and of your clients' businesses plus plain old 'Murphy's law' will combine to create enough excitement and variety for any normal human being. If you can reduce the number of variables and minimize the potential impact of each one, you should expect to save time and wasted work so that you can focus your efforts on winning profitable business from clients that are a pleasure to work with. The process of planning and gathering information so that you can better understand your business environment achieves just that. There used to be a saying among Special Forces personnel: 'Plan rigorously; execute ruthlessly.' The result is to reduce risk.

Planning is a necessary precursor to action. It is not a substitute for action. The best of plans will make no impact if they are not implemented. That is especially true in the case of sales activity. Nothing happens in any business unless someone sells something. There is much to be said for what some people call 'the Nike approach' – just do it. However, the probability of success is increased by sound planning; hence an alternative approach: 'DTFW' – roughly translated as 'Do The Work First'.

Action plan overview

To keep this relatively simple, I have divided the action plan into three streams of work:

1 Marketing and positioning.
2 Sales activity and client relationships.
3 Business systems.

These streams of work can be undertaken almost in parallel but the marketing and positioning stream must be started first because its early stages inform the work that will be done in the other two streams. The content of each stream is summarized in Table 11.1. (If you would like to have a complete over-view of this plan in spreadsheet form, you can download a copy from the website associated with this book: **www.professionalsbusinessdevelopment.com**. You will find this plan under the Downloads tab on the navigation bar.)

Before you can make a start on Streams 2 and 3, you will need to have a reasonably clear idea of the following elements of Stream 1:

● Context (Chapter 1).
● The factors that define your 'perfect client' (Chapter 2).
● How you wish to define your role with those perfect clients (ie the value that you will uniquely deliver (Chapter 3 and elements of Chapter 4).

These between them serve to define the range of commercial fit opportunities for you with your perfect clients. Everything else flows from these factors.

It is essential to understand that these factors are not static. They are dynamic and change over time. Economic conditions alter. Your experience grows over time as (one hopes) will your expertise and ability in your chosen field. Your ability to work with other clients, perhaps larger firms or at a more senior level or across more geographic locations, will change. If the size of your firm changes or you form strategic alliances, these will alter the context in which you operate. These factors need to be reviewed reasonably frequently (say once each year formally as part of your business planning process, with an interim, half-year 'checkpoint'). There should in any event be an immediate review if a significant change occurs in any one of these factors.

An obvious example of a significant change would be the collapse in 2008 of Lehman Brothers. That should have sparked an immediate and in-depth review of their business context by every professional service firm regardless of location. Sadly it did not and, even several months later when the world was in the grip of a major recession, I had senior clients in the professions telling me that the situation was no more than a metaphorical bump in the road and that things would swiftly return to the way they had been in 2006/7. It was a variation on the view of those who in October 1914 said that World War I would be over by Christmas.

It is worth spending a little time on these initial definition activities. The context should be reasonably clear in terms of macro-economics. As regards industry-specific factors and their possible impact on client firms, these may well require some research and indeed some conversations with clients and potential clients to understand their industry from their standpoint and their perceptions of their position in it.

There is no substitute for simply allocating the necessary time (it is after all an 'A' task) and just doing it. The work need not take long; probably only a couple of hours if you know a reasonable amount about the industries in which your perfect clients operate. If you lack that knowledge, clearly it will take longer, but even if you start from scratch it should not need more than two days of effort to create a viable picture if you use the resources readily available online and in print. A conversation with a knowledgeable client will save considerable time and give you the benefit of real-world experience. However, it is wise to test that experience-based view against what you find elsewhere; ideally there should be a high degree of correlation. If there is not, more work is needed.

In any event, set a fairly short time limit for this initial context research and stick to it: avoid the temptation to imagine that doubling the volume of additional information adds a similar degree of value to your understanding. Experience indicates that this is very rarely the case. In any event, as mentioned above, these factors are dynamic, so it makes little sense to try to fix a perfect picture in amber.

Having carried out the initial context definition, you can now begin to work on the three streams in parallel. If you are a solo-preneur, clearly you will have to work on one issue at a time, but you can switch between streams on a logical basis if you use the timeframes outlined in Table 11.1. If you have the benefit of colleagues, you can divide the work between you to gain concurrent activity but only once the initial definition work is done. It sets the parameters for everything else and it is important that everyone involved buys into the results.

Action plan to-do list and timings

This section breaks down each of the three work-streams into a more detailed set of action items. Against each action item is shown with a 'Day by when' figure. This is simply designed to indicate where in the overall process each action fits, beginning with a notional Day 1 start date. The benefit is to allow you to see the sequencing. Clearly the actual time allocation depends on the resources available to you and the stage of your business; a new start-up will not need to invest much time initially in planning and running meetings, but will need to invest more in identifying perfect clients/commercial fit opportunities and developing collateral material, for example.

TABLE 11.1 Action plan in three streams

Stream 1: Marketing and Positioning (See Chapters 1, 2, 3 and elements of Chapter 4)		
Key elements	**Sub-set of activities**	**Day by when**
Context	• Exercises in Chapter 1	1
Your perfect client and your chosen role with that client	• Exercises in Chapter 2	1
Your brand and brand management	• Values and behaviours for which you wish to be recognized • How you wish your clients to see you • Areas in which you add great Value to clients	2
Positioning as an expert	• In what areas do you seek to be recognized as the 'go to' person by your clients? • How to evidence that expertise (examples: writing articles for trade journals, write a book, etc)? • Make a plan to enhance your perceived expertise and allocate time to execute that plan	2

TABLE 11.1   *continued*

Developing your collateral material	• Develop a list of existing and prospective collateral (eg, articles/case studies) • Allocate time to collate, update or write from scratch • Plan how you will use each item	3
Fee scales (generic base structure)	• Work out basic fee per day of delivery needed to ensure break-even • Base this on revenue required and a realistic estimate of actual delivery time likely to be achieved and not on time theoretically available • Allow for holidays, administrative tasks, marketing and selling activity • Assess costs to allow you to calculate 'outcome based' fees or the 'rate for the job' (ie outputs not inputs)	4
How to relate those fees to the Value you deliver? **Note:** *this is a generic process that needs to be adapted for each client because no two clients are exactly alike. This process gives you a robust starting point and helps you to understand what you need to charge for your services in order to remain in business*	• Determine the benefits and results that your perfect client is likely to seek (based on the problems they are likely to experience, weaknesses they may need to overcome or strengths they need to leverage with your help) • Consider the process of delivery (how you will deliver if the client hires you) and assess the cost to you • Add a profit margin and an allowance for contingencies • Round up that overall number • Define a total rate for the job and test it against the benefits/results for the client • Ensure that the benefits to the client exceed the sum of cost plus hassle by a wide margin • Decide how to explain that to the client in terms that will immediately resonate and can be visualized	4

TABLE 11.1   *continued*

Stream 2: Sales Activity and Client Relationships (See elements of Chapter 3, Chapters 4, 5, 6 and 7)		
Key elements	**Sub-set of activities**	**Day by when**
Locating the right clients ('target acquisition')	• Identify professional/trade journals likely to be read by your perfect clients. Subscribe	3
	• Identify industry conferences and seminars	3
	• Book a place or offer to speak	7
	• Identify and join industry forums online and offline	6
	• Identify and join industry networking groups	8
Developing your 'knock-out self-introduction' to answer the question 'What do you do?'	• Follow the model in Chapter 3	7
	• (Your perfect client, their problem or dream, how you help)	
How to extend your professional network?	• LinkedIn: set up a complete profile	8
	• Make a plan to ask for referrals from current contacts	onwards
The relationship pyramid	• Assess where you are on the pyramid with each current client	7
	• Build a plan to move up the pyramid for each client	8
What drives the client? Emotional drivers Buyer types and roles Learning preferences	• For each current client, identify the commercial fit	7
	• Assess what drives the primary buyer at the level of personal needs and psychological needs plus learning preference	8
	• Identify the other buying role within the client firm and carry out the same exercise	9

TABLE 11.1 *continued*

Planning and running meetings	• Make it mandatory in your firm to complete a meeting planner for each face to face meeting and phone call with a client	9
	• Sell the benefits internally	
Referral generation	• Based on your knock-out self-introduction, write a short description of the Ideal referral for you	7
	• Where possible identify individuals to whom you want to be referred (as opposed to introduced)	9
	• Make a list of current contacts that can offer referrals	10
	• Make a plan to seek referrals	10
	• Follow up on each one	ongoing
Fees versus value (Review and reality check against competitors)	• Work out your cost to do business	7
	• Identify the level of revenue needed to cover the cost to remain in business including paying salaries and other on-costs. Add a profit margin	
	• Based on an achievable level of delivery time over the coming year, calculate the revenue needed per day of delivery	
	• Identify the likely value to the perfect client of the successful resolution of the commercial fit issue you identified	
	• Ensure that the value you deliver is greater by a margin than the necessary cost and within the ballpark of competitors' fees (too low will kill your business: too high will hinder take-off in the early stages	8

TABLE 11.1   *continued*

Writing great proposals (or letters of confirmation)	• Prepare a small number of template letters following the outline in Chapter 7 using generic benefits and results statements and based on a small number of generic commercial fit ideas	10
	• Prepare appendices covering items such as process of engagement, timings, fee arrangements, cancellation terms, etc and standard terms and conditions	12
	• Have these checked by a lawyer if required	14
Strategic accounts: • Which clients must be treated strategically? • How to do so?	• Identify current clients that are of sufficient importance to be treated strategically based on the factors in Chapters 7 and 9	20
	• Identify the individuals in the key buyer roles for each client firm plus what drives each one, etc	
	• Identify how to move your relationship with each individual up to a partnership level	
	• Plan the role in which you wish to be seen by each client ('Be recognized as ...')	

TABLE 11.1 *continued*

Stream 3: Business Systems (See Chapters 8, 9 and 10)		
Key elements	**Sub-set of activities**	**Day by when**
Quality assurance process	Develop a generic QA process: • Identify the factors that drive success for each project and how each is to be measured • Develop a generic process for communicating within the project team and with each of the key buyers at the client firm • Agree that process with the client for the project in hand • Diarize key milestones and plan backwards so that you can pre-position all communication prior to any formal oversight committee meeting • Design procedures to ensure that your team operates a 'no surprises' culture • How to hold team members accountable for delivery	20
CRM systems and processes	• Identify what information you wish to capture and how it is to be used • Ensure that the process of capturing that information is part of 'business as usual' not a separate, manual process • Plan how to keep the data current • Clients • Past clients • Prospects	12 onwards
Knowledge management/ 'precedents'	• Design systems in conjunction with CRM and with same design considerations in terms of keeping data current, etc	13 onwards

TABLE 11.1   *continued*

Collateral management	• Define basic set of 'collateral' documents such as case studies, etc	14 onwards
	• Plan usage such as website, blog, articles for trade press, etc	
	• Develop website to include data capture (name and e-mail address in exchange for download of collateral items)	
	• Add to auto-responder update mechanism and link to CRM system	
Document management	• Define process for document filing and links to client records	15 onwards
	• Link documents to CRM system	
	• Plan version control	
	• Define document sharing protocols	

Mapping things out

Whether you will do the work solo or as a group, I highly recommend that you invest in:

- A flipchart – old-fashioned it may be, but it is still one of the most powerful tools in business, in my view. (Once, having captured a client's ideas and agreed actions on a flipchart sheet, I asked him to sign it to confirm his agreement to the actions and the timings. He immediately back-tracked until we agreed that they were simply what he had said. He signed the sheet and, to the surprise of his colleagues, the actions were carried out on time.)
- Several packs of large Post-it® notes of different colours.
- A roll of brown wrapping paper (as wide as you can find; say 80–100 cm).
- A pack of BluTack.
- A set of marker pens (I prefer the chisel tips because you can achieve a fine line where necessary).
- A roll of clear sticky tape.

The benefit will be that you can brainstorm as a group, capture ideas and put them up for the whole team to see. Capturing ideas on a flipchart makes them easy to grasp because they are visual. The brown paper can be BluTacked to a blank wall and Post-its® can be used to create flow charts (for mapping processes) or value chain diagrams. The Post-its® can be repositioned as necessary. Different colours can represent different processes so that you can map out how different elements interact. Once the process map is agreed and final, the Post-its® can be taped in position so that they do not become detached when you move the strip of brown paper. You can then capture the final version in, for example, PowerPoint®.

If yours is a new business, you have the luxury of designing it from scratch and building the systems you need for today and (within reason) for the future.

IT platform: a side note

As a sidebar, to the extent that you need to use IT systems, I recommend that you use established software from mainstream providers that is proven to work on the computer platform you have chosen for your business. The basic platform choice for your end users is between MS Windows and Apple. Of course, you could use one of the Linux variants as your operating system but, while it may be intellectually interesting, it is likely to cause all kinds of compatibility problems for you and for clients. Each has advocates and the use of Apple Macs is growing in businesses beyond what was once their core community of graphic designers and media folk. In my view there is no single 'right' choice for a given business, but you should certainly opt for one or the other, rather than try to run both side by side as it will minimize IT support requirements and cost.

That said the default for most businesses is Windows as the operating system with MS Office as the main software suite. It is perfectly viable to use open source software such as Office Libre (formerly Open Office), which has the benefit of being free of charge, so long as you are able to send documents to clients that are compatible with MS Office. Few things are more frustrating for a client than to receive a document in an unfamiliar file format that they cannot open. Even something as basic as 'zipping' or compressing a file to reduce its size for sending by e-mail can cause problems if the client lacks software that can unzip or un-compress it. Many will simply delete the file rather than download the relevant software online – even if it is free of charge.

The right people

The growth of any business will be limited if it does not have enough of the right people either as employees or as trusted external contractors. Making sure that you have them is therefore a critical element of your implementation plan.

In this penultimate section of the book, therefore, we explore how to recruit the right people for your business (or for your team if you are part of a larger organization). We also look very briefly at organizational structures and some of the pros and cons of hierarchy, a flat structure and a matrix organization. The structure of your organization will have an impact on the kind of people you need to recruit so it is worth considering the two in tandem. The ideas on recruitment are also relevant if you are a solo-preneur who needs to bring in associates for a given project.

Many business leaders talk about the idea that 'our greatest asset is our people'. It may be true (it is not always so) but few senior executives act as if it is and fewer yet recruit people as if it were the case. Too many firms follow the approach of a client firm of mine where the senior partner remarked ruefully that they went to great lengths to gain 'lateral hires' (senior people joining the firm from outside) only to find that these new joiners did not integrate with the rest of the firm and, often, failed to achieve the additional business that had been expected. He observed that it was like buying expensive house plants and forgetting to water them. I replied that it might be a case of putting tropical plants into a garden suited to hardy perennials.

If the conventional wisdom is that people are the greatest asset of the firm (and Jim Collins among others has produced comprehensive research indicating that it should be so) one should also consider the corollary: that they can also be the greatest source of risk in all its forms. That is arguably of increasing importance the higher up the organization one goes (look no further than the cases outlined in Paul Babiak's book *Snakes in Suits* ...).

All businesses need good people. Even as a solo-preneur, you will from time to time find a need to bring in colleagues, whether as associates or simply by way of outsourcing part of a project that you cannot deliver adequately (or choose not to). It is vital that the people you select are aligned with you in terms of values and behaviours (or the 'way you do business') and probably more so than their sheer technical ability.

If you are part of a larger firm the impact of poor recruitment (ie where the selected candidate is not aligned in terms of culture with the rest of the team, regardless of skills set) is somewhat diluted. However, the impact of such people can be tremendous in a smaller firm. It is often said that individuals join a firm because of the boss and stay because of their colleagues. The reverse can also be true if the colleague proves to be toxic. Interestingly, one of the most common reasons cited for leaving a job is incompatibility between the employee and their boss. It would appear that the initial attraction wears off and indeed can reverse over time at work, as in personal relationships. Most recruitment processes follow an approach that focuses on competencies and skills and relegates values and behaviours/culture to a poor third place. In other words, conventional recruitment is a case of:

- recruit for skills set;
- select for perceived (or tested) competence (and perhaps being 'like us');
- hope for appropriate attitude.

A better approach (and one that has served the military well for many years) is to:

- recruit for attitude;
- select for aptitude;
- train for skills.

In many ways a good recruitment process follows an approach similar to that described earlier for identifying and engaging with 'perfect' clients. The factors that will attract great people to your firm will be similar to those that attract great clients (and only rarely will technical excellence be the overriding factor). In my view, it doesn't matter whether you are recruiting an additional member of your own team or someone to work alongside you as an associate; the thought process is very similar.

Start out by answering, for a given job role, the question: 'Given all that we know about our business and our preferred clients, what would be the traits and characteristics of a "perfect" candidate for this role?' If you are working as part of a team, it is helpful to involve the whole group (regardless of seniority) in brainstorming the answers. Capture them on a flipchart so that everyone can see them and build as necessary. That exercise need not take more than 10–15 minutes.

Summarize the answers you have (which will typically focus on values and behaviours rather than skills) and add a short list of essential skills and/or qualifications. From this you can develop a one- to two-page description of both the role and the preferred candidate, which can be used to brief a recruitment consultancy or prepare an advertisement. Don't forget that, if you work within a larger firm, it will usually be helpful (indeed it may be mandatory) to look at internal candidates first.

You can now break down the role into its component responsibilities and summarize in bullet point form what factors/criteria would describe excellent performance in that aspect of the role. I use a table in Word to do this, set out in five columns in landscape layout. The first column sets out the relevant criteria. The second shows against each criterion a couple of bullet points that describe what 'excellent' performance would look like in that role for that criterion. The third describes in the same way 'satisfactory' performance and the fourth factors that would indicate 'development needs'. In the last column where possible I add a note of how those 'development needs' can be met.

It may not be helpful to look at an existing incumbent in a similar role elsewhere in the firm; start from scratch and consider what 'good' would look like in the abstract. So far as possible, relate your criteria and the description of performance in each criterion to the desired experience for the client.

The benefit of this approach is that it helps to speed the 'on-boarding' process of any new staff member; they can easily see what is expected of them and know how their success will be judged. When it comes to periodic performance evaluations, the staff member takes a copy of the sheet describing their role and marks the bullet points against each criterion that they feel best describe what they have delivered. You do the same on your own copy of the same sheet. Before you meet to talk about performance, you exchange sheets so that the discussion can focus on points of difference of view.

In addition, I ask each person to write a few sentences that describe what they think has gone well over the relevant period and what they feel could have been done better or differently and, if they have feedback for me, to provide it on the same basis. I also ask them to list a few key things that they have learnt over the period. The benefit is that evaluations become less conflicted and indeed in most cases staff members evaluate their performance less highly than I do. The process is also transparent and the use of an objective set of criteria depersonalizes it.

Costs of recruitment

In any recruitment scenario one factor that needs to be considered is the cost of employing the person that you prefer for a given role. In searching for additions to your team, think carefully whether you wish to employ them or hire them on an 'associate' or 'contractor' basis. Either way, within reason, in my view, cost should be a minor consideration, provided that the attitudes, values and behaviours (or traits and characteristics) of the individual appear to be congruent with your own and those of your firm, and the individual either has relevant experience and a proven track record (where that is necessary for the position you have in mind) or appears to be eminently trainable and willing to be trained.

In this context there are five levels of training/development:

1 Fully trained.
2 Under-trained.
3 Untrained.
4 Unwilling to train.
5 Un-trainable.

Ideally one would recruit at Level 1, but it rarely possible to do so unless one takes an internal candidate for a given role. That is a double-edged sword. Although the individual will no doubt know 'how we do things in this firm' and therefore require less training in your firm's processes and procedures, it may prove to be a barrier if you wish to make changes to the way the firm operates or to its culture. An external candidate has the advantage of no pre-conceived ideas in such a situation.

Those at Level 2 or 3 may well be fine so long as you are willing to invest in the necessary skills development and the necessary traits and characteristics are clearly present. Individuals who appear to be at Level 4 or 5 should be avoided; to try to work with such people is in my experience akin to pushing water uphill – hard to do and deeply frustrating.

When considering the cost of employing an individual (as opposed to hiring them as an associate/contractor), don't forget that salary is only a small part of the overall cost. Additional elements will typically include:

- some form of employee insurance contributions (National Insurance in the UK);
- pension contributions;
- healthcare contributions;
- office space (unless your firm operates from a 'virtual' office).

In addition, it may be necessary to provide benefits such as a company car or car allowance depending on seniority and role and perhaps a guaranteed minimum bonus for the first year, plus in some cases dedicated support staff such as a PA. The total cost of employing an individual is often assessed as double the cost of the base salary. If you use a recruitment agency or 'head hunter' to find staff for you, their fee will be additional and will often be of the order of 30 to 33 per cent of the first year's package (as opposed to base salary). For an employee on a salary of £50,000, with a guaranteed bonus of £25,000 and other benefits totalling £15,000, the fee to a head hunter would on that basis be £27,000 to £30,000.

In many cases it will be cheaper to hire an associate/contractor and there is an added benefit in minimizing your fixed costs even if the variable cost (the contractor's fee) is higher in the short term. If you wish to take on an employee, consider whether the person you are thinking of hiring will be able to generate new business in their own right or if you will have to generate sufficient business to keep all your staff fully occupied.

It is also necessary to take into account things such as the cost of office space and support staff. These costs vary quite considerably depending on location. Even within a relatively small area the cost of space and the salaries of support staff can vary widely. However, many professional firms (especially smaller ones) are taking advantage of the option for staff to work from home through the use of technology. This can save considerable cost overall and also offers greater flexibility for your staff in terms of the timing of work as well as location.

There is of course an up-front cost in providing the necessary technology at the home of each staff member (if they are employees). However, there is a benefit for the individual in saving commuting time, being at home when children return from school, etc. In some cases, firms may agree that a full-time employee can become a contractor working for them, say, three days per week with the remainder of their working time able to be allocated elsewhere. In addition, there is a potential benefit in reduction of carbon emissions due to less time spent travelling. All of these are factors that many employees find attractive. By contrast, many who adopt this approach say that they miss the social interaction of an office environment: the 'coffee machine conversations'.

Surveys carried out by firms such as British Telecom, which uses flexible working patterns and remote working, indicate that output is if anything somewhat improved in terms of both volume and quality relative to a conventional, office-based approach. However, the use of this type of work pattern requires a change of mind-set on the part of the leadership of the firm as well as on the part of staff; it takes a significant degree of trust on both sides to move to an approach where hands-on supervision is not feasible. The key is to measure output not presence (ie, simply being in the office). It becomes a matter of deciding what factors are key drivers of success in your business and how to measure them for the benefit and reassurance of all concerned.

And finally...

If a fish ceases to move forward, no water will pass over its gills and it will die from lack of oxygen. If you lose momentum on your business development activity, your business will eventually die for lack of revenue.

In this book, you have a toolkit that can help you to build a successful professional practice, whatever your field of work. Like a gym membership, it will do no good unless it is used and you work at it. Business development requires activity on your part – and particularly in identifying, locating and making contact with the right kind of clients for you and your firm. The aim of the toolkit is to help you to focus the activity so that it can be as productive as possible and the productivity is profitable. The absolute requirement for success is that you persevere and do some work each day towards building your business rather than simply delivering for current clients, which is all too tempting. Even if I am hard at work on delivery for a client, I will always take at least 20 per cent of each working month for business development.

Many sales professionals think in terms of building a 'sales funnel' or a 'pipeline' of work. I prefer to think in terms of identifying the people I would like to bring into the funnel as a more important activity and hence one that demands more time. Once I have identified them and confirmed (by asking the right questions) that there is a genuine commercial fit (ie, I can help them) and that the individual is someone with whom I want to work, it is relatively easy to begin to articulate value, etc. Rather like lawyers in court who never ask a question unless they are pretty confident they know the answer, I try to avoid having a 'business closing meeting' unless I am confident that there is a fit, that I have established a basic personal connection with the client and there is a budget available. The result is to minimize the likelihood of rejection and save a tremendous amount of time.

FURTHER READING

Collins, Jim (2001) *Good to Great*, Random House, London

Ferrazzi, Keith (2005) *Never Eat Alone*, Doubleday

Gawande, Atul (2009) *The Checklist Manifesto*, Metropolitan Books (Henry Holt), New York and in paperback in the UK by Profile Books, London (2011)

Johnston, Peter D (2008) *Negotiating with Giants*, Negotiation Press (through Baker & Taylor,)

Kahneman, Daniel (2011) *Thinking, Fast and Slow*, Allen Lane (Penguin Group)

Koch, Richard (2007) *The 80 / 20 Principle*, Nicholas Brealey Publishing

Miller, Michael (2009) *You Tube for Business*, QUE (Pearson Education)

Reed, Jon (2011) *Get up to Speed with Online Marketing*, FT Prentice Hall (Pearson Education)

Rutledge, Patrice-Anne (2010) *Teach Yourself LinkedIn in 10 Minutes*, Sams Publishing

Scoular, Anne (2011) *FT Guide to Business Coaching*, FT Prentice Hall (Pearson Education)

Shih, Clara (2009) *The Facebook Era*, Prentice Hall (Pearson Education)

Timperley, John (2002) *Network Your way to Success*, Piatkus Books

RESOURCES

The website that supports this book is **www.professionalsbusinessdevelopment.com**.

By clicking on the Resources tab in the navigation bar you can gain access to downloadable versions of many of the planning tools and exercises in the book, including:

- The Meeting Planner
- Score Sheets
  - Perfect Client score sheet
  - Client View score sheet
  - Client Mapping score sheet
  - Client Firm Relative Positioning score sheet
- Templates and Issues
  - The AAR template
  - Questions to consider before reorganisation or other major change
  - Implementation plan overview
- White Papers/Focus Notes
  - Seven Reasons Why Meetings Fail (and how to avoid them)
  - Trade Show and Conference Success
  - Five Reasons Why Collaborations Fail
  - Strategy: Key Questions

Other tools, templates and White Papers will be added in due course. Sign up to be notified when new material is added to the website.

INDEX